Ali
ENJOY REP
Teresa

A FOUNTAIN OF HOPE

A STORY OF LOVE, COURAGE
AND
HOW HIS EYE IS ON THE SPARROW

by

TERESA PETKAU

Heart Beat PRODUCTIONS INC.

A FOUNTAIN OF HOPE

Published by
HeartBeat Productions Inc.
Box 633
Abbotsford, BC
Canada V2T 6Z8
email: info@heartbeat1.com
604.852.3769

Cover photo: Teresa Petkau
Cover design: Dr. Carrie Wachsmann

ISBN: 978-1-895112-56-6

Printed in USA

DEDICATION

This story is dedicated to all of those who hunger and thirst for righteousness – and to those who have prayed for many years to see our city and region transformed in a way that will see unity and love prevail.

This book is also dedicated to the one I love, my Saviour who first loved me: Jesus Christ. He wooed me as a young woman in my late teens. My life was transformed from that time.

This story of hope is also lovingly dedicated to my three precious children: Christopher, Michael and Summer.

And, of course, this is written in honour of a man who loved me dearly, and loved those he encountered daily: my late husband, Bert Petkau.

Bert, you are always close to us, and you will never be forgotten.

A FRIEND COMMENTS

One day a few years ago, as I was happily working away at my desk, my phone rang. There was a rather soft-spoken stranger on the other end and he wanted to know if I would like to meet for lunch. A few days later, when the lunch appointment arrived, I met Bert Petkau for the first time.

As we talked that day, I soon discovered that our hearts were made from the same cloth. We had similar dreams, experiences, and passions for worship. We quickly became friends, and for the next couple of years we met frequently.

A short while later, Bert became sick, went into the hospital, and never came out again. I was heartbroken by his loss. Rarely do you come across a person in life with whom you form such a quick bond.

Shortly after Bert's memorial, I met Teresa, Bert's wife. Together with a group of friends, we spent the better part of the next two years praying together every Thursday night. I soon realized that Teresa had the same heart for her city, prayer and worship that Bert had. I count it an honor to have known these two - Bert for a short period of time, and also Teresa as she has walked out different stages of her healing process.

This book flows out of that journey. There is healing contained in the words you are about to read, healing that proceeds from a heart that is intimate with the presence of Jesus. Let it wash over you as you catch a glimpse into the lives of the Petkau family.

Dean Maerz
Worship Pastor, New Life Church
Abbotsford, BC

CONTENTS

INTRODUCTION

I regularly meet people who have suffered loss, felt disappointment with life, or experienced difficulties that they weren't expecting. Perhaps you are one of them.

Not in a million years did I think I would go through an experience that would so suddenly change my life forever – let alone that I would write a book about it.

This chronicle is a true account; the testimony of one love story ended too soon, and another story of faithful love that never ends.

It is the story of the wondrous workings of the God I know called "Abba" (an Aramaic word that means "Daddy"). He is a loving Father who meets us in our most troubling circumstances, and stays by our side to comfort and heal. I pray that my testimony of walking out of despair and into hope, will encourage you.

Welcome to my journey and I encourage you to ponder and meditate upon the scriptures, and devotional thoughts relating to my story as well as some of my poems, and lyrics from Bert's music. I've included links to the songs Bert wrote, so that you can listen, and perhaps enjoy them as much as I do.

– **Teresa Petkau**

His Eye Is on the Sparrow

Why should I feel discouraged?
Why should the shadows come?
Why should my heart be lonely
and long for heaven and home?
When Jesus is my portion,
My constant friend is he;
His eye is on the sparrow,
and I know he watches me.

Civilla Martin, 1905

"Civilla Durfee Martin (1866-1948) was born in Nova Scotia and died in Atlanta, GA, USA. In *His Eye is on the Sparrow* (1905), she has provided one of the most influential and often-recorded gospel hymns of the 20th century."

by C. Michael Hawn, *His Eye Is on the Sparrow*
***The Faith We Sing,* No. 2146**

CHAPTER ONE

DESTINY UNFOLDING

The first thing I remember was waking up on the side of the road with a blanket wrapped around me and a woman praying out loud for me. Although I didn't understand what was happening at the time, I felt peaceful, and then lost consciousness again.

It was the year after I graduated from high school, and the young man I was dating was driving me to a party in his MGB sports car. We had left his parents' home in Delta, B.C., and were driving much too fast along Canada Way towards Burnaby. It was a dark night, very foggy, and we hit a curve in the road. The sports car went out of control, slid across the road, and crashed into a telephone pole.

The next morning, I regained consciousness in Emergency at the Royal Columbian Hospital in New Westminster. On impact, the gas cap had come off and gas was leaking into the driver's side of the car. We were fortunate that the car did not blow up. My friend was seriously injured and stayed in the hospital for months. The crazy thing was that I walked out of the hospital the following day with only bruises on my legs and minor gas burns on my face.

A year and a half later I gave my heart to Jesus Christ and I had a powerful experience being filled with the Holy Spirit. My heart was opened to a peace I had never experienced before.

Not long after that my mom, my sister and I were invited

to a prayer meeting in a home in Surrey, B.C. I noticed a woman across the room eyeing me like she knew me, but I didn't recognize her. When the meeting was finished, she came over and asked me if I had been in a serious car accident a year and a half before. She was the woman who had put a blanket over me and prayed for me.

She told me she was a nurse, and that she had just finished her shift that night and was going to head home on her usual route. She had a strong urge to go down Canada Way instead, and I'm so glad she did. We hugged each other joyfully, and I was filled with gratitude.

This was the first time I realized that God does have a plan for each one of our lives and that He watches over us even when we don't know Him yet. God saved me that night, and began leading me towards my destiny: life with my husband Bert, and my eventual journey into hope.

Psalm 19

From the hands of me
comes a hope that shines within.
It's in my heart again,
like a gentle flowing stream.
This I know is real, yet I am amazed. This I know is true.
The heavens tell of Your Glory, Lord, the skies of Your great mercy, Lord.
The earth cries out, You are holy, Lord. Mountains bow down, oceans reveal
Your power and majesty.
From the end of the age
your love was present then,
surrounded by Your mercy.

Bert Petkau, *How You Made the Stars* CD, Jan 2002.

Hope Nuggets

A path of new discovery is hope being unveiled.

CHAPTER TWO

FOUNDATIONS

There was no indication of cancer coming our way when Bert Petkau and I met at Northview Community Church in the early '80s. It was the spring of 1984, and my brother-in-law, Perry, was working in a men's clothing store selling high-end suits. Bert went in to purchase one for his sister's wedding and happened to get into a discussion with Perry about a new church that was being established in the area. Not long after, Perry, my sister and I went to check it out and started attending on Sunday mornings.

I was young and single and wanted to get married and have a family some time in my future. I had been living and working in Vancouver, and was a brand new Christian. To get grounded and disciplined in my new walk with God, I had decided to move to the country. My mom was a nurse at the hospital in Abbotsford, and I thought that might be a good place to live. I packed my things and moved out to the Fraser Valley.

I met Bert one morning at church when the service was finished, and we had a casual, friendly conversation. Over the next few years, I got involved in a young people's group and prayer time before the services started, though there were many Sundays I could not attend because of my job. During the week many of us attended a Bible study where we developed friendships and community.

One day at a church retreat, Bert was leading the music and needed someone to write out the songs for the overhead projector (doesn't that date a person!). He asked if I would do that, as my handwriting was neater than his, and my organizational skills a little more evident. While Bert was leading us, I opened my eyes to see him passionately worshipping God – and Cupid shot an arrow right into my heart. I knew he was the one.

I had a conversation with God, that if this were of Him, He would work it all out and draw us together.

Over those few years, Bert lived his life working in construction and going overseas to help in worship settings for different mission organizations. He was asked to play bass in a band called "Titus," a talented group that did concerts in England. The band members even found their way to Berlin before the Communist wall came down in 1989. He was a busy guy even in those days, and often seemed like his head was in the clouds, but not in a scatterbrained way – it's just that he was always an idea man!

Bert was also the original Northview worship leader, and during his spare time, he wrote an interdenominational musical called, "His Majesty Exalted," a drama featuring a choir and a choreographed dance. Bert was ahead of his time – nothing like this had been done before in the region.

We had become friends by then, and to promote the musical we handed out flyers around the city in the evenings after work. The first performance was at Central Heights Church in Abbotsford, and because of the show's uniqueness, it attracted a lot of attention. The musical was well attended and performed in various settings in 1986 and 1987, and it became a catalyst for unity among the churches.

I sang soprano in the choir, and our friendship developed to the point where we both knew God was drawing our hearts together. In the summer of 1987, after the last performance,

Bert and I began dating and a special love grew between us.

We had been going together only a few months when Bert showed up at my apartment with his guitar in hand. I was so surprised when he opened the case, produced a bouquet of red roses, opened a ring box, knelt down on one knee and asked me to marry him! When I said yes, he took out his guitar and sang a song he had written just for me.

I was commuting to the city for my job, and he was working with a friend building houses, but we managed to plan a wedding in just four months. And on November 7, we exchanged our vows of love. I wrote the words to a song on my lunch break one day, which Bert put to music and sang to me on our wedding day.

We moved into a little, two-bedroom apartment after our honeymoon and began our journey together – marked with God's presence and a deep love for one another. As I look back, I am amazed at how God does give us the desires of our hearts, and how faithful He is in every season we walk through in our life's journey.

It was an adventure for sure! Life with Bert: dreaming, creating, inventing, and sharing his gifts and talents along the way with others. This world needs each of us to give a smile to someone else, to show kindness and to be exactly who we were created to be. Life with this gifted man not only put a smile on my face, but also on the faces of many others along the way.

Our Song of Love

I'm your lady, you're my man.
What God had designed is His perfect plan.
Lord, take this love you have breathed,
Whisper it softly throughout our beings.
Your tender touch brings life to my soul.
The Creator's love shines over us whole.
Lord, blend our wills, our hearts, our minds,
To be transparent, untainted, and kind.
Capture, oh God, our every whim,
That unspoken thoughts would never grow dim.
May the window of your love so sweet
Reflect the strength of the hand I meet.
Be the keeper of our souls,
Evertrusting lambs in your enfold.
Love so gentle, Love so true,
May our eyes be focused on you.
Take these servants you have called.
Melt our dreams, our hopes, our all.
We give thanks to you above.
We draw our strength from your perfect love.

lyrics: Teresa and music: Bert

... And if one prevail against him, two shall withstand
him; and a threefold cord is not quickly broken.
Ecclesiastes 4:12

Teresa and Bert
November 7th 1987

The Deepest Part

All along the waterfall
Things are feeling right
But sometimes it's hard to see
Things that can hinder you
Things that make you stumble
Things you just don't see.
Many are the words we find
Many are the dreams
Many are the songs we play
Many are the streams that flow
Many shades and colours bleed
Shades and colours bleed.
It isn't hard to be free,
oh I believe, oh.
'Cause eyes can't see, oh
'Cause it's from the heart.
So sing it out, oh
Sing it loud, ooh
Sing it out, oh
From the deepest part
'Cause it's from the heart.
Things that I would not believe I can almost see
Though my heart is fainting
These storms don't bother me
They won't change the way that I feel
The way I feel
The way I feel.
'Cause love will always find you
Love will always see you through
'Cause love will always find you
The past is far behind you
The future's right in front of you
The past is far behind you
Love will always see you through.

Bert Petkau, *Seven Songs*, 2011
https://soundcloud.com/bertpetkau

Hope Nuggets

Hope is an adventure waiting to unfold.

CHAPTER THREE

BUILDING ON A ROLLERCOASTER

All adventures have their challenges though, and the ups and downs of Bert's career in the building industry taught us many lessons about life. We learned in our trek to pray about which jobs we should take, and which ones we should let go of that could cause us problems – a continual learning curve in the construction business.

Many years ago, we learned one particular lesson when we were having challenges with a high-rise project in Vancouver. Bert and I communicated about everything, so it was no surprise when he told me we were losing our shirts on this job. But he was an honest man of integrity, which is why he drove to the city every day and gave it his all, even knowing we were bleeding money. Our crew did everything they could to rectify problems, but it seemed to be too late.

When Bert shared the bad news with me, I was struck with fear and uncertainty. Bankruptcy? Wow! We never dreamed that would happen to us! What would happen to our family? Our children, Chris, Summer, and Michael, were quite young at the time.

I can still remember that day vividly. Bert went off to Vancouver to do what he could; I got down on my living room floor and cried out to God. I told Him I was scared - what was going to happen to us? As I lay prostrate before

Him, I thanked Him for allowing us to live in our beautiful home – and whatever happened, I was okay with it. I was learning to surrender.

Suddenly a peace came over me, and I sensed that somehow things were going to work out.

Bert shared with me that we had to see bankruptcy lawyers the following week. He told me how he and his partner Ruben had been in a restaurant discussing their bleak circumstances. They prayed together and surrendered the situation to God.

Bert said a peace came over them, as it did for me, and there were tears when they shook hands and left the restaurant, trusting God for whatever came next.

When Bert got home from work that Friday night, we began getting ready to go on one of our regular dates. He told me he had to submit a bid for a job before we went out, and he faxed it off to the general contractor.

The following Monday, he received a phone call from the contractor asking where the bid was for this particular job, as bids were now closing. Bert told him he had faxed it on Friday and that it should already have been there.

The next day, the contractor called Bert again, and said that his quote had fallen on the floor by the fax machine, adding, "Come in, we want to talk with you." Bert went to the meeting, and found out that his was *not* the lowest bid – *but he got the job anyway!*

This was truly God's favour! We saw His sovereign hand in our situation. It was a wonderful project that enabled us to pay off our debts in a very short time and still come out ahead.

I'll never forget that day, and I give thanks for the lesson in surrender that God taught us early in our marriage. He does take care of us in every situation as we look to Him and trust. It is something I do now with child-like faith every day of my life. *My future is in His hands.*

His Love Is Over Me

I am weak – I am faint with love.
Strengthen me again, with your love.
Lead me near, lead me to your side,
To the one that my heart loves.
'Cause His love is over me.
His love is over me. His love is over me.
Your mercy, your love is ever over me.
Winter is past, the rains are gone,
Flowers do appear again.
The sounds of singing lead me along,
To the one that my heart loves.
'Cause His love is over me.
His love is over me. His love is over me.
Your mercy, your love is ever over me.
Your love is over me. Your love is over me.
Your mercy, your love is ever over me.
I am weak – I am faint with love.
Strengthen me again, with your love.
Lead me near, lead me to your side
To the one that my heart loves.
His love is over me.
His love is over me. His love is over me.
Your mercy, your love is ever over me.

Bert Petkau, *Seven Songs*, 2011
https://soundcloud.com/bertpetkau

Hope Nuggets

Hope is waiting, having to be patient in
uncertain times.

CHAPTER FOUR

GOD LOOKS AT THE HEART

In 2010 it was so nice to finally get a local job just down the street from where we lived at the time, building the High Street Mall in Abbotsford. Over the years, our projects had either been out of town or spread across the B.C. Lower Mainland.

It was a big job for us! Thinking back, it is amazing that it is not 60 meters of concrete, but 60,000 meters that now sit on the property! A lot of concrete pumps were needed, and a lot of rebar was used to facilitate safety. I smile to myself when I see the "big-box" stores, boutique outlets, and other retailers and restaurants there, and remind myself that we built this modern-day shopping and entertainment landmark.

One day, Bert was walking across the impressive 13 acres of property that would eventually become the mall. Rocks, stones – and more rocks and stones – lay in the foundations at this early stage. With his usual hard hat, work boots and safety vest on, and with his cell phone glued to his ear, Bert was busy strategizing how to make the job go better.

He was navigating the sea of pebbles and stones, talking on his phone when he happened to kick a rock and go on. He stopped, turned around and went back, bent down and picked up one smaller, particular stone. It was shaped like a heart, so he slipped it into his back pocket.

Bert knew I loved anything heart-shaped. At suppertime that night, he lovingly handed me the stone that I still have as a reminder of the mall we built. How thoughtful he was. Even in his constant bustle, his heart found time for mine. I so appreciated this about Bert.

The gift of this stone also reminded me that God watches over us, and looks at our hearts. I've always wanted my heart to represent Christ's heart to people. My goal is to stand before my Maker one day and to hear Him say, **"Well done my daughter. You were faithful with the measure of love I gave you, and you gave it to others."**

Somehow it is the simple things in life that put a smile on my face – even a simple, silly, heart-shaped stone! I am forever grateful.

CHAPTER FIVE

MEANT TO LIVE IN THE VALLEY

In the midst of that long building project in February 2012, we were looking at various places in the Lower Mainland to build a family home once again. Our adventurous spirits had us driving to Vancouver, Langley and White Rock, looking for the perfect spot to build – or even just the right house to buy. We thought we wanted a change from living in Abbotsford, and we were open to moving somewhere else.

After many weekend drives to different areas, I remember coming back from White Rock and chatting away. As we were sharing together, we were suddenly both taken off guard; looked at each other; and realized that we were thinking the same thing: God had placed us in Abbotsford for a reason. The Holy Spirit wanted to do something in us and through us. He was making it clear that we had been planted in the Fraser Valley with a purpose all those years ago. We were builders in the natural and builders in the spirit. He was going to give us a vision for what that meant. But for now, we knew that *we were there to stay.*

CHAPTER SIX

LIGHTS AND OCEANS

Besides the construction business and all that went with it, Bert continued to be deeply involved in worship and writing music. He led worship in many different settings and had recorded a few albums through the years. So many significant and meaningful relationships came from this side of Bert's life.

It was around May of 2012 when our friends Andre and Steph Antonio moved from Chilliwack into our basement suite in "Abby." We moved Bert's office upstairs so Andre could establish a professional studio in one of the downstairs rooms. Bert had just written a song called "Lights & Oceans", and shared with Andre his vision for a new album based around it. Andre loved the idea. For the next two years, they collaborated, prayed, and put their best into this work, which in turn became the best of Bert's five albums.

Bert and Andre spent many hours working on the music, and the two of them would have amazing conversations that were sometimes more meaningful than putting down tracks and lyrics. They would often come upstairs for dinner or coffee, and we had great laughs and discussions together. One of my biggest smiles came from the gorilla slippers that Andre wore throughout the recording of the album.

Andre and Steph are an amazingly gifted couple, and the

four of us soon became good friends. We were family as Bert and Andre worked together, and we all shared life together. Circumstances threw some curveballs into Andre and Steph's relationship, but through prayer, counsel, and friendship, they overcame their obstacles and thrived.

I remember on August 26, 2013, Bert's birthday, that I picked up a cake for him, and we had a little celebration together at home. I have kept a little phone video from the day of Andre playing his ukulele, with Steph and I singing a very "Happy Birthday" to the birthday boy.

A few months later, our friends announced that Steph was pregnant and expecting their first child. Baby August arrived on August 1, 2014. It was a significant month for the four of us: the birth of new life, and the birth of an extraordinary album that will always have a special place in our hearts.

We will treasure the photos of little August, with his big brown eyes and precious smile, being held by Bert in his hospital bed.

Bert and I treasured the years we lived life together with Andre and Steph. They brought such joy to Bert's heart and he loved them. God's timing for them being with us, and being involved in the creation of the album was completely perfect. And then, it was a new season in their lives, and new doors were opening for them elsewhere.

I will always remember Andre, with his Brazilian accent, and Bert the Canadian, both faking British accents while recording!

"Cheerio!" they would say.

I can just imagine Bert looking down from heaven and smiling over his good friend, calling him "mate" in his best British impersonation.

Further to Freedom

Every time the wind blows, my heart begins to feel.
Then it leaves me wondering
Then it leads me here.
Still your love finds me
Through this darkened veil
Then it leads me to your door.
I feel it when I'm near you.
When you come near
When you come runnin'
When you come close beside
I'm further to freedom.
Holding on to what I've known,
Holding on to what brings me
Further to freedom.
Promises within –
They're everything I need.
They don't leave me wondering
They don't leave me here
And I find myself just waiting.
I look to you alone.
You've opened up my heart again.
You've opened my eyes.

Bert Petkau, *Lights & Oceans*, 2014
http://www.soundcloud.com/bertpetkau

Hope Nuggets

Hope is music stirring the heart strings to worship.

CHAPTER SEVEN

MUSICAL CELEBRATION

In June 2014, Bert and I were so excited getting ready for the release party for *Lights & Oceans*. All the time and effort spent with Andre and Steph, and many other local musicians, brought expectations of joy that evening. I went early to set up food and beverages, and to make sure all the goodies were ready for when we had a break between sets.

My girlfriend Moira and I had reacquainted on Facebook, and I was excited she was driving out from Vancouver with a friend for the party. We had both grown up Catholic in the '70s, and when we finished high school those many years ago, life took us on different journeys. Who would have thought that 35 years later we would reconnect at a music event for my husband?

It's interesting how our friendship re-established after all those years. God had a plan. Moira and I have had many wonderful walks and talks since then, and we keep in touch. The night of the party, there were many others, young and old, from different churches who showed up to help us celebrate.

I love how Bert loved life to the very fullest, and he was not afraid to step out and fulfill his dreams – even if it meant mistakes along the way. He lived life well. At one point during the party performance, he surprised me by putting his acoustic guitar down and coming to me in the front row. He took my hand for a slow dance to the country song he had written, **"If I Could Fly."**

I am not one who likes the limelight – but that was a special dance with a special man on a special night. I will always be blessed to soak in the songs he wrote and to hear his voice in each of them. I am so grateful to have such a unique thing: Bert's music. It will always be vital to our family, and to a lesser extent for everyone who embraced his love for God and enjoyed his music.

There is so much giftedness out there, and I've learned that it's important to celebrate one another and to bring out the best in each other. God is no respecter of persons; we all are his favourites.

Ron Peters

If I Could Fly

If I could fly up to the hills
If I could sail on distant seas
If I could feel the way you feel
I would understand.
I would understand your heart.

I would feel you close, right here with me.
I would feel your heart.

When I feel you I see again the light that's in your eyes.
It's the light that's in your eyes.
The light that's in your eyes.

Sometimes I feel those shadows rise again.
Sometimes I don't know which way to turn.
If I could feel the way you feel
I would understand.
I would understand your heart.

I would feel you close, right here with me.
I would feel your heart.

When I feel you I see again the light that's in your eyes.
The light that's in your eyes.
The light that's in your eyes.

Bert Petkau, *Lights & Oceans*, 2014
Listen on www.soundcloud.com/bertpetkau

Hope Nuggets

Hope is a song birthed by love.

A Moment In Time

Won't you come away with me, my love, my darling one?
I am taken by the beauty in your eyes, I see your heart.
Is it you I'm searching for? Is it you my heart longs for?
Could it be something that's burning deep within,
Could it be true?
The day I realized it was you, it was just like yesterday.
A moment out of time.
In the midst of the storm through the pain, it was something inside,
And it was in my heart to find.
A moment in time.
Was it real or was I blind? Was I hoping for a sign?
Or was it something I could find? Was it true? Was it you?
The day I realized it was you, it was just like yesterday,
a moment out of time.
In the midst of a song through the pain,
it was something inside, and it was in my heart and mind.
A moment in time. A moment in time ... was in my heart to find.
A moment in time.
Like a river is the heart that sings –
it flows from your heart, it flows from your heart.
And like the ocean, how vast it seems.
How great is your love. How great is your love!
It's like a river flowing. It's like a wind that's blowing.
It's like a song that comes from the heart
That isn't too complicated, or too hard to play,
'cause it was there from the start, and it comes straight from
the heart,
heart, heart.
It's like a river flowing. It's like a wind that's blowing.
It's like a song that comes from the heart
That isn't too complicated, or too hard to play,
'cause it comes straight from the heart, and it comes straight from
the heart, heart, heart.

Bert Petkau, *Lights & Oceans*, 2014
https://soundcloud.com/bertpetkau

CHAPTER EIGHT

CALM BEFORE THE STORM

The year 2014 began with our love still growing, inventions being birthed, dreams being fulfilled, and the prospect of seeing God create new visions in our hearts.

Bert was in his routine, busy being the "idea man" full of fearless adventure. He was my kite, soaring into the sky and boldly pursuing new heights. He would occasionally come in for a landing to carry out his latest endeavours. Life was good – we were blessed and we were grateful.

We had eventually found property in Abbotsford, built our new home, and moved in at the end of March, tucking away 17 years of memories from our old place in West Abby. Our children were now young adults, and for the most part, living independently and figuring out what life had to offer. Our oldest son, Christopher, was married to Sarah, and they had been living in North Carolina for the past three years.

I remember their beautiful wedding in North Carolina which took place on property belonging to Billy Graham's family. We could sense such peace and authority as we strolled toward the rustic cabin that belonged to Graham's grandfather. What a privilege to watch Chris and Sarah exchange their vows on that porch before God, family, and friends! It was one of the best days of our lives.

Chris and Sarah came home for their yearly visit in June

and announced that they were planning to move to Canada. We were delighted and thought that perhaps Canadian grandbabies would be coming soon. I still have a room in my house filled with my kids' toys, stuffed animals, and our daughter's old, single bed. People smile when they walk through that bedroom and see signs of my faith to be a grandmother one day.

Meanwhile, Summer was attending Columbia Bible College and working part-time. Michael was living in Vancouver, working full-time in construction and attending the B.C. Institute of Technology part-time, pursuing a career in construction management.

For Bert and I, our Friday night dates of 27 years continued on a regular basis. We turned our cell phones off, shared the mysteries of life, our dreams, our love for one another, and the hurdles we had cleared over the years. We also wondered: What does God have in store for us in the next season of life?

Bert would get up early Saturday mornings to take our pup, Lucy, for a hike up nearby Sumas Mountain. He would talk to God and spend time in nature, quietly seeking the Father's heart. We both loved God, and it was important for each of us to have daily private time with Him. The stillness, peace, and quietness of His presence carried us through the bustle of life.

It was now summertime, and one Saturday afternoon we decided to look at commercial buildings in this town where we knew God had called us to stay. We jumped into Bert's black Tundra, driving around to check out sites. Why? The vision that we knew God was going to give us had come! We wanted to see a 24-hour prayer house and worship centre established.

Our area is known as the "Bible belt" of Canada, and God had brought us here in our younger years from opposite ends of the country. Bert was from a really small farming community in Port Rowan, Ontario, and I hailed from Vancouver, B.C. It's amazing how the Holy Spirit can touch two hearts living in distant provinces, and in His perfect timing unite them as one in a single city. We didn't know how the pieces of the puzzle would fit together, to see our dreams come true – but we knew we wanted to establish something that represents unity within the body of Christ and in the city.

Never Ending Love

I hear it in the night. I listen to the sound.
I feel it in the music. Your love, it's comin' down.
I will lift my heart to you, give my all to you.
I'll sing about your never-ending love.
I'll sing about your never-ending love.
When I think of your great love,
I can feel you comin' closer to me.
In the presence of my God,
There's no greater pleasure.
Here in this place,
Where I find your never-ending love.
I see it in your eyes. I see it in your heart.
I could not describe your love. I couldn't even start.
I will sing my songs to you. It's in my heart to do.
I'll sing about your never-ending love.

Bert Petkau and Chris Janz, *Soldier Boy,* 1998

Hope Nuggets

Hope is the fragrance of love in the air.

CHAPTER NINE

BERT'S DREAM

Copied from Bert's computer

About five years ago, I had a very interesting dream. It seemed to take me from my life, where it was at that time, through a maze of prophetic scenes I did not understand. As the dream began, I found myself walking down a road looking for a means of transportation. As I made my way down a path, I ended up going through a very dark tunnel that was quite narrow at one point. The scene began to change, and it seemed like I was entering into a different world.

At one point in the dream, I came to a rock face where I saw an ancient archway that was completely barred shut. I felt compelled to enter the dark opening in spite of the solid, iron grid in front of me. As I entered, the steel structure gave way and seemed to disappear before my eyes. I saw a set of stairs winding upward, and my curiosity moved me forward. As I began to ascend, the stairs became like new, and the steps were easier to negotiate.

I suddenly found myself on a moving escalator! It turned into a moving platform on what seemed like a skyway overlooking a great city. As I looked down from the platform, I saw a very large number of people around tables on the next level below – it was a banquet of supernatural proportions. Then, without any warning, I found myself in what seemed like a roller coaster that was much faster than anything I had experienced in the natural.

I would normally get sick on a thrill ride of this intensity, yet I was fascinated by the ease of the speed and acceleration I was experiencing. It was very exhilarating as I witnessed sudden flashes of light with colours all around me.

I never woke up from this dream, but the next day I remembered it. Dreams like this came to me for the next several months, and I made it a practice to write them down.

I am a dreamer when I am asleep and when I am awake. My life is full of imaginations, and "what ifs?" I love to search out the mysteries of God. As I observe God's children, I see the attributes of our eternal Father.

There is no better way to understand His ways than to look into the eyes of the sons and daughters of the living God. Though we live in a fallen world, we have a treasure that is worth far more than any treasure found on this Earth. It is worth more than all the silver and gold that exists on the Earth and in the Earth.

This hidden treasure is to know the one we call the lover of our souls, the one who holds the keys of death and Hades, the one who grants us immortality, the one who gave his life for all mankind, the one who holds everything in the palm of his hand.

CHAPTER TEN

THE DAY OUR LIVES CHANGED FOREVER

One beautiful September afternoon in 2014, I stood on our balcony admiring the beauty of Mount Baker. Bert had gone to the hospital that morning because he was not feeling well.

I thought he would be home shortly, as he had been to the doctor's many times for stomach pains that he learned to cope with over the years. He had been diagnosed with Irritable Bowel Syndrome long ago, but through a somewhat healthy diet and regular exercise, he was able to manage his condition.

The hours ticked by that day, and I realized – looking at Mount Baker in front of me – there was something wrong. I looked to heaven and felt this warm peace come over me, like a preparation or a warning that this time it was serious.

Bert walked through the front door seven hours after he had left. He had a concerned look on his face, and I knew somehow it involved the "C" word. We held each other and cried, and cried, and cried out to God for help! When life hits you out of nowhere, what do you do? We could hardly breathe. We gathered our thoughts and beseeched God for His mercy.

Fear, like we had never known, gripped us those next three nights – but we would not give in. We prayed and stayed close to God and each other. A journey I was not prepared for was ahead for my family.

The following Monday we went to the oncologist for the results of Bert's CT scan. The news was Stage 4 colon cancer with some spots on the liver. Hope welled up inside of us when the doctor said they could deal with the spots on the liver, and chemotherapy would probably take care of the colon. We phoned Chris and Sarah, and Bert's sister Lorraine who flew out from Ontario to be with us all.

The following Tuesday, just eight days later, I got a call from the physician – they needed to do immediate surgery on Bert's colon. An hour later, the hospital called us to the emergency room, and we were stunned by the news we heard: In just a week, Bert's liver had become engulfed with cancer! My husband also had a perforated bowel, free air in his abdomen, and he had developed pancreatitis.

Lorraine, my children and I stood there in disbelief. There were many tears as we were told that there was nothing the medical staff could do. We were advised to go home and get our things in order. The suggestion was that Bert had two months to live. Those next few weeks, we prayed together, trusting God to heal Bert. We never gave up on that.

———————————————————

I reflected back upon the day in June when I felt strongly to organize a surprise party for Bert – his 59th birthday was coming up on August 26. My idea was unusual, as you would typically plan for a surprise 60th; not a year earlier.

August 26, 2014, arrived with a surprise for Bert and delight for everyone. Friends from around the province came to celebrate Bert on his special day. Our friend Ron Peters, an expert photographer, took spectacular shots – moving memories my family and I will always treasure.

Chris and Sarah were stunned when Bert and I phoned them with the cancer diagnosis. They packed their belongings and drove four days across the continent, crossing the border into Abbotsford the first week of October.

Time stood still as we felt our world falling apart – yet our difficult journey as a family was just starting. My life changed forever almost overnight. I went from being a cared-for wife to being my husband's caretaker – even giving him hydromorphone shots for his pain.

I was desperate to get his body more alkaline. Both my nutritionist and naturopath worked diligently to come up with healthy combinations to cleanse Bert's system and organs. Day after day, we worked together, coordinating what he should have for breakfast, lunch, and supper. No matter what healthy diet we devised, it was futile against the scourge of pancreatitis.

I felt so helpless, asking God to give me strength for each day. The seconds and minutes barely seemed to move on the clock. When the pain was very bad – with a smile on his face and those blue eyes looking back at me – Bert would pick up his guitar, write a tune, and worship God, his Saviour. Somehow the comfort of the music distracted him from the pain.

Day and night, people would come by to pray for him and encourage us. On October 14, Thanksgiving Day, we called our children together for a family meeting. Bert had spent the morning on his computer and most of that afternoon going through scriptures that applied to our children's lives. He wrote words of encouragement for them, and later that evening I sat quietly in the recliner with tears running down my cheeks as I listened to him speak a blessing over each of our three kids.

When he was finished, Michael rose from his chair, walked over to his dad, put his hand on his shoulder and told him he was a good father, and that he loved him. It was the last Thanksgiving we would celebrate as a family.

Blighted Hope

Tears gently flow down my cheeks,
my eyes wet with grief.
I taste the salt, despair stained upon the
corners of my mouth.
Devastation is looming like a lion seeking its prey.
The unknown cold and distant
aches chill within my heart.
Oh God, where are you in my suffering!
I hear your stillness in the pain –
Come rescue this shattered heart.
I lay it down. I let it all go.
Your outstretched hand in my lament,
Dry my tears and comfort my sorrow.
Let hope rise again in the depth of my soul.

By Teresa Petkau

Hope Nuggets

Hope is strength in a desperate situation.

CHAPTER ELEVEN

SOLDIER BOY

I remember the day I took Bert to the insurance office to change our vehicle into my name. He sat slouched over in the chair as I did my best to focus on the paperwork and put the new plate on my car. My heart went out to him, as every little movement seemed to cause him pain. I could see how helpless he felt. He was so incredibly brave. I was so unsure and afraid.

One Friday in mid-October, we invited some friends for supper. Lane Luxon hooked up a high-tech microphone to his iPhone and with care recorded Bert's testimony: Bert shared his story of faith and sang the last song he would ever record, "Crimson Waters." I was grateful Lane cared so much to capture Bert's singing. Bert sang with passion through his pain, and when Lane posted the video on YouTube, many people were touched by his raw honesty. [1]

Not long after that special evening, Bert's pain was increasing and I could no longer care for him at home. He was unable to eat or keep nutrition in his system, so he was admitted to the hospital. I felt so helpless, yet relieved at the same time – what else could I do?

[1] http://www.dreamcity.org/?s=Petkau)

We were a couple who loved being together. Sometimes we would flip a coin to decide where we were going on a date – then off we'd go, looking forward to the night's adventure.

Now all had changed. The craziness of coming home to a dull silence after long days at the hospital – and sleeping alone without my man to talk to – was paralyzing. But it was preparing me to trust God every step of the way through this journey. In those days at the hospital, we could truly feel the presence of Him, knowing we were enveloped in prayer, support, and love. The Holy Spirit gave us a supernatural peace that we desperately needed every day.

Dr. Stewart Brown, our palliative care specialist, would have weekly meetings with me, girding me for the days ahead. He said my husband was like "a rock star" with so many people coming to visit, pray, and love on him. I shared with him our love for God, and that we also believed in His healing power.

Dr. Brown was a man of faith and respected our deep commitment. All the doctors and staff at Abbotsford hospital were so kind, selfless and caring.

It didn't stop there. A man from Rwanda who was in our city ministering heard of Bert's illness and came to the hospital to pray for him. Emanuel Tuwagirairmana laid hands on Bert and spoke a simple prayer of healing.

Emanuel's visit was special because he himself had experienced a miracle of recovery: Pronounced dead in 1994, he came back to life after seven days, as in the story of Lazarus. Yes, it's true – and after this miracle, his whole town of Gitarama came to know Jesus Christ. Emanuel now travels the world sharing his testimony and experiencing the joy of seeing many come to know Him.

When Bert was still at home in October, friend David Kim flew all the way from South Korea to stay with us for a week. He fasted some meals and faithfully prayed day and night for Bert. We were honoured to have him.

Other pillars and committed friends – Doug and Suzie Watts, Judi and Phil Bowler – faithfully came to the house and the hospital to pray for Bert. We all believed for a miracle of healing, as many around the world were standing with us in prayer.

Word of Bert's illness had also spread through the construction industry, and some of his work colleagues came to our house to connect with him and encourage him. They knew the business side of Bert, but when he picked up his guitar to sing through his pain, they marvelled with teary eyes.

Bert's life was a testimony to many. The outpouring of support for him reminded me how much of a light he was, and how well respected he was in his field. Countless other friends and family showed up at the house and hospital to stand with us on our journey.

I had prayed for others to be healed physically and had seen it happen. It was our turn now – *we needed a miracle!*

Crimson Waters

I will look to you, my friend.
I will wait for you, my love.
Living waters, flowing down from above.
Gentle words flow from your heart.
Words that strengthen every part.
Healing waters flowing down, again.
With love as strong as death for all to see.
A love that knows no bounds,
it's over you and me.
Crimson waters, flowing down – because of your love.
Because of your love. Because of your love.
Words and music by Bert Petkau

Filmed October 17, 2014, by Lane Luxon.
YouTube: https://www.youtube.com/watch?v=ATscwMA5bgg

Ron Peters Photography

Hope Nuggets

Hope is the anchor that allows the storms of life
to cease.

CHAPTER TWELVE

IN SICKNESS AND IN HEALTH

My daily life at this point was mere survival. I retreated to the gym or out for coffee with a friend when I wasn't bedside with Bert. I was trying to keep my head above water. The long hours each day felt like never-ending seconds slowly ticking by. Some days my mind swirled, wondering what the outcome of all this would be. I cried out to God for mercy and strength, trusting Him that our miracle was coming.

But in the midst of the worst times, I also experienced precious moments with my family. I am a grateful woman, so I appreciate the life I've experienced – especially the past 30 years of my journey with Bert, Christopher, Michael, and Summer. The privilege of being a wife and mother has been the highest calling of my life. I look at my children and will always see the love of Bert in and through each of them.

One evening around suppertime, I got back to the hospital after a nap at home. Michael was sitting in a chair across from his dad, reading scripture aloud to him from the Book of Job. I sat quietly, with tears in my eyes, listening to father and son share an intimate, spiritual connection. It is one of my many treasured memories.

Before he fell ill, Bert and I had planned a special holiday for that year's wedding anniversary. On November 7 we were going to return to Puerto Vallarta, Mexico, where we honeymooned 27 years earlier. Now it was not to be, but I still wanted to do something for Bert on our special day, knowing he could not leave the hospital.

I searched at home and I found our four hour, 1980s VHS wedding tape. It showed everything: getting ready beforehand, putting flowers on the vehicles, arriving at the church, the ceremony, taking photos, the reception – it must have been an 80s thing to record every aspect with a video camera! Our friends Brian and Kristen Olynick brought a small television to the hospital for me; Lisa and Rachel LeGear gave us a romantic, custom-made basket of goodies; and Bert and I sat together in his cramped hospital bed with a cozy blanket and battery-lit candles to relive our wedding day.

I will never forget the paradox of love and pain we experienced that day in Bert's room. Our love story was real. Summer came to visit and took a photo of us crammed onto the bed celebrating – a snapshot of our long relationship.

Marriage is a gift, through its ups and downs. God makes us all different individuals, with different perspectives and different ways of viewing things. It can be like 'iron sharpening iron' if we allow the differences to help one another, and to learn to understand each other.

When our kids started to hit the teen years, the cracks in our marriage began to show. We had different ideas on parenting – I thought it was important to have clear boundaries for behaviour that we stuck to, and Bert was much more easy going. Bert was also working full-time, leading worship in various places, and very busy. We knew we were struggling and thankfully we both saw that we needed outside help.

We quickly found a counsellor, and began four years of getting the help we needed to understand each other better, and also get tools for raising the kids together as a team. For the first time, we really began to gel in our relationship and experience deep peace together.

Bert and I learned to refill at the "grace tank" (his term) or the "grace station" (my term). When we didn't see eye-to-eye, we would remember what Christ's grace did for each of us. Grace is the unearned favour of God. God extended his forgiveness to us when we didn't deserve it, because He loves us. It was important that we learned to overlook some things in the day to day of living together.

Bert and I would sometimes say, "On this one, we need to agree to disagree," or, "Let's go to the grace station." And the matter would be settled!

It became important on our date nights to take time to clear the air. We would talk through the things that were bothering us, solve problems, forgive and be forgiven, and then move on to having fun and appreciating each other.

I remember Bert saying to me not long ago, "I love you more, Honey, in these later years as we are getting older." Why? Because we realized that through the trials and joys, we were growing together. We had learned to value all we had been through as a team.

I am so grateful that both Bert and I were committed to solving our problems and learning to look at each other from God's perspective, with eyes of love. I realize that what we had together was very special and that's what made this sudden, shocking crisis even more difficult to bear.

Love Like This

Never really ever had a love like this.
A gift so precious, a love so real.
To do it all again, you know I'd take the risk.
There's no love like this.
I've always had a reason to depend on you.
Whenever we're together, it's all I can do.
I never have experienced a heart like yours.
There's no love like ours.
And when I look up to the skies
And see the distant stars on high
The truth is never hard to find.
And when I look into your eyes
I get this feeling deep inside
Of precious moments that are mine
Our love is fine
Never really ever had a love like this.
A gift so precious, a love so real.
I've finally come to realize how much I've missed.
There's no love like this.

By Bert Petkau for Teresa Petkau
***Soldier Boy*, 1998 Produced by Chris Janz.**

Holy Splendour

Early in the morning before the dawn breaks forth,
I sit silently in the quiet of the night.
Waiting, pondering in stillness, my spirit longs for you my love.
Deep unto deep in the calm of the night.
Your light rises over me above the mountain top,
As a curtain slowly drawing — your presence is revealed.
In the hush in the stillness, you make no sound.
Unforeseen, your presence appears in an unexpected way.

By Teresa Petkau

CHAPTER THIRTEEN

LAST DAYS IN THE HOSPITAL

Day 55 – Friday, November 14

I found myself standing at the nursing station, again asking Dr. Brown: "How long has Bert got?" He said Bert was a fighter and had a strong heart, even though we knew his kidneys had shut down and his liver was overcome with cancer. His colouring had changed from a pasty white to yellow, and much of his body was bloated.

"Teresa, he could live another day or another week," Dr. Brown told me.

I thanked him and plopped down in a big, leather chair by the nurses' station. I knew in my heart, short of a miracle from God, my man would soon be leaving this Earth and going to heaven. I was dazed to think of not having him here anymore. The cold, numbing reality of not having another 20 or 30 years with the man I loved weighed constantly on me, no matter how I tried to ignore it.

We had imagined seeing our children get married. We had prayed to become grandparents and to grow old together, and we loved travelling together and hoped to do more of it.

About 15 years ago, Bert looked at me and said, "One day, Honey, I will take you to Paris." And that dream came true for our 25th anniversary. It was a trip of a lifetime that took months to plan. We ended that adventure at Wimbledon in London. Bert loved to play tennis, and we enjoyed watching it on television, so it was an amazing experience to see the pros playing on the grass courts, in person.

After that, a trip to Spain in 2015 had been our hearts' desire – to see Antoni Gaudí's famous structure, the Basílica de la Sagrada Família in Barcelona. Bert was inspired by great architecture, and with the help of our brilliant foreman Peter Unger, had incorporated distinctive curves into some of his projects, such as the Surrey library.

I looked back, treasuring the adventures that we'd had, and realizing that the dreams for more in the future were quickly disappearing.

I also thought of the times my boys would phone their dad to run things by him. They might seek counsel about something personal, but it was always because they respected his opinion. They just wanted to talk to their dad.

With tears in my eyes, I questioned: "Would our lovely daughter Summer ever walk down the aisle with her daddy, holding his hand on her wedding day?" My mind raced to so many things that day, wondering what the future held. There were so many "what ifs" at this crucial moment. It seemed so unfair, so fast and unbelievable, what was unfolding before us as a family.

I know life isn't fair at times, yet this was happening to an exemplary man. Reality was screaming in my head: My "idea man" was soon, perhaps, going before his allotted time. Confidence turned silently into helplessness as I watched what was happening.

Day 56 – Saturday, November 15

Cancer is a cruel disease. It ravishes a person not only physically, but also mentally as it progresses.

Bert was no longer able to get out of bed, and the nursing staff lovingly shifted his positions to make him as comfortable as could be. You could see the drugs were taking a toll on his body (though helping with the pain, I presume). He was unable to eat anything solid. He had his routine: crunching on ice chips in a cup; then sipping small amounts of his "go to" Gatorade and Pellegrino sparkling water.

A month before, when I saw him unable to eat or keep anything down because of the pancreatitis, my heart was devastated. Now, I realized my husband was truly dying and there was nothing I could do – except pray. I had nowhere else to go, except to God.

My heart hurt so badly, I felt myself drowning in shock and sorrow. I did my best in the 58 days of "fight or flight" to be strong for my children, and to be positive whenever I was around Bert. Numbness was descending into deadening disbelief, though in our hearts, we hung on to hope for a miracle of God's healing.

It was now evening, and some of my extended family came to see Bert in the hospital. He sat up anxiously in the covers – then pitifully begged each of us to help him out of bed, which for his safety, he was no longer allowed to do. With those big, blue eyes and a flirtatious smile, he scanned the room from person to person, hoping someone would give in.

My husband, soul mate, best friend and life partner looked to me for compassion. He motioned me to come close, and I knew he wanted to latch on and swing himself off the mattress.

I kept my distance. None of us would help. We tried our best to calm him down, repeating some version of the same cerebral excuse: that he might hurt himself if he escaped his bed. How frustrated he must have felt – and how abandoned by those who supposedly loved him most.

My sweet little niece Julia, who was about six, shyly sang

a song in German she had just learned in school. Bert was still "with it" and he beamed ear-to-ear as we clapped for her jingle. But now it neared 10 o'clock when he would usually settle in for the night. It was time to leave, and one-by-one we gave Bert a hug and kiss before going.

I was almost out the door when he firmly called my name. Exhausted, I went back to the chair across from him. There was a weary silence in the room, but suddenly Bert looked intently at me – straight into my eyes – and said, "Honey, I love you."

I said, "Honey, I love you too. I'll see you in the morning."

I gave him another hug and peck on the cheek. Spent with fatigue, I went home and collapsed into bed.

Day 57 – Sunday, November 16

I arrived at the hospital around 9 a.m. to find my love in a coma. Tears streamed down my cheeks in a silent room, save for a humming machine that pumped medication into his body. Somehow, I knew Bert could hear me, but there was no response of any kind. Through sobs, I was touched to realize that I was the last person he spoke to here on Earth – and his last words were, "I love you."

Thank you, God, I will always be grateful for that. The night before, I had prayed on my knees. "Please do not let Bert pass away alone, or without family by his side." Now I wiped away my tears and sat silently holding his hand.

Day 58 – Monday, November 17

The next day I walked into Bert's room, listening to his breathing in the stillness of our surroundings. I had no idea if he would live another day or another week, and I spoke again to Dr. Brown, wondering how much time we had left.

A couple of hours went by, and for some reason, I felt compelled to call our foreman, Peter. I phoned from the hallway and asked him to send my boys to the hospital. They were on a building project of ours in south Surrey, so I knew it would take time for them to get here.

Now, Summer and Sarah were at Bert's bedside. My boys arrived not knowing their dad was in a coma, and tear ducts burst. I knew our lives were changing forever. Without thinking, I blurted out: "Kids, are you able to release your dad and to let him go to heaven to be pain free?"

Stunned by it all, they exclaimed, "Yes!"

We were now sobbing, but among the tears and anguish, we each spoke to Bert, pouring out our hearts – how much he meant to each of us. We released him into the Father's arms, and to be pain-free.

I felt to sing two hymns: "Nothing but the Blood of Jesus" and "How Great Thou Art." We struggled and sang off-key, missing the worship leader who always helped us. The peace in the room was evident, yet bittersweet because of what was soon to happen.

The afternoon was passing by quickly. My children and I stood around Bert in silence, listening to changes in his breathing. The prayer from the night before was about to be answered. Chris remarked that his dad's breath was getting shallower and shallower. And two minutes later, at 4:35 p.m., our family watched Bert exhale peacefully for the last time.

"Rest in peace my love. We will meet again in eternity. You will forever be in our thoughts, and you always will be loved."

Bert Petkau was a man of great integrity who loved God, his family, and countless others who loved him in return. He shone the love of Jesus Christ wherever he went. He left a remarkable legacy that will continue on through us and others. Bert's death was not in vain, and one day we will understand why he passed too soon.

Nothing Can Hold Me

You've won my heart. You've drawn me near.
Though now, in part, you're never distant.

I'll find my way back near to you.
'Cause in your light, I can feel your love, again.
'Cause nothing here will ever hold me.
Nothing here will ever hold me from you.

'Cause your love means more than what words can say,
Much more than what songs convey.
It's everything I could hope for.

Through the storm I know there's a light.
Through the fire I can feel you.
And when my heart grows faint, lights become dim.
And when I feel your song, I can feel your love, again.

'Cause your love means more than what words can say,
Much more than what songs convey.
It's everything I could hope for.
And it's my freedom to know
Your kindness leads me to your heart.
It's your mercy that draws me near,
Your forgiveness instead of fear.

Nothing can hold me here. Oh, nothing can hold me here.
'Cause your love means more than what words can say,
Much more than what songs convey.
It's everything I could hope for.

It's my freedom to know
Your kindness leads me to your heart.
It's your mercy that draws me near,
Your forgiveness instead of fear.

Nothing can hold me here. Nothing can hold me here.
Nothing can hold me, can hold me, can hold me.
Nothing can hold me, can hold me, can hold me.
Nothing can hold me, can hold me, can hold me.

Bert Petkau, *Dream*, 2011
https://soundcloud.com/bertpetkau

Hope Nuggets

Hope is an arrow that heals a shattered heart.

CHAPTER FOURTEEN

THE MORNING AFTER

I thought it was over, but I awoke the next morning in a stupor, having to plan a memorial. I could hardly think, let alone organize myself to prepare my husband's celebration of life.

Fortunately, Bert had left us with a plan. He had specifically instructed us on how he wanted his memorial to be, if his healing did not come. In those long days at the hospital, we had discussed in detail matters of the heart, our business, my future and our children's.

With Summer, Chris and Sarah, family and friends, we organized the event within days. In spite of my numbness, I knelt down the night before and asked God to be glorified at Bert's memorial.

When it happened on November 27, everyone involved was those he had requested. Vic Schellenberg helped us all relax and engage by recounting funny stories of his days as Bert's roommate before they both married. Good friends Norm Strauss and Kenny Rahn led worship and played some of Bert's music. Special tributes were given by Ruben Friesen, Ken Greter, Alistair MacArthur and Brian Olynick.

Through it all, I sat between my boys. Their presence and their strong hands in mine comforted me and gave me the strength I needed to make it through the service.

I was amazed that people had travelled all the way from Vancouver Island, the Okanagan, Alberta, and Ontario to honour Bert, even though it was winter. Many said that it was like a mini reunion to see those from various churches we had been involved in. Over and over again we heard the theme that Bert represented unity and love within the church and the community.

Two rows of construction management and employees sat among the 900 people who came out to honour Bert. Among them were a well-dressed elderly Indo-Canadian man and his son, whom we rented a yard from to store our equipment and construction forms.

A week before Bert passed away, these two had come to the hospital to visit. I was in the room that morning when the old gentleman walked in and seemed so shocked at Bert's condition. In somewhat broken English, he said, "I just saw him in July. He would stop his truck and roll down his window and say hello to me before he left the yard ... He looked well. What happened? He was a very nice man!"

The father and son spent a few hours in the hospital with me as I shared our journey and how we were coping. I'll never forget Gary, the young man, sitting in silence. He looked up at me and asked, "How are you so strong?"

I shared with him the love of God that Bert and I carried in our hearts; that it gave us the strength to carry on. I gave him one of Bert's CDs, and he sat quietly reading it from cover to cover.

When it was time to leave, the tearful father gave me a hug and said again how he had appreciated Bert taking the time to greet him at the end of a workday. Wow! Sometimes it's the simplest acts of kindness – or perhaps it's Jesus' love within in us reaching out to others – that touch lives. I, in turn, was touched that Gary and his father had come out to honour Bert.

Another guest from the construction world at the

memorial was Ahmed, an Iranian engineer who was filled with the love of Jesus. He later shared with me that one of Bert's colleagues had approached him after the service and asked, "How do I get from being a Catholic to what that man represented?"

I told Ahmad: "Please tell him, Bert's wife was also raised Catholic. You don't need a priest to receive forgiveness and redemption. It's a personal relationship through what Jesus Christ did for us at Calvary."

Bert, in life and now in death, was a signpost to the love that God has for each of us. He was genuine and caring, even in ways I did not know. He ministered to so many people behind the scenes. I learned that day that many people were grieving with us, for a man they so loved.

Never Alone

Sometimes I just don't see
There's so much more
Sometimes I just don't feel it
The way I should.
There's a river in my soul and I'm never alone.
Oh, Oh, Oh.

Maybe you can try and change me
Even if you could
Maybe try and make a way.
All I know is
There's a river in my soul and I'm never alone.
Oh, Oh.

Feel the higher ground
Feel His love around
It's like a river and it's coming down
It's really coming down.

Oh, Oh.
Da da da da da da da ah ah
It's like a river and it's coming down
It's really coming down
It's really coming down.
Oh, oh, oh, oh, oh.

Bert Petkau, *Lights & Oceans*, 2014.
https://soundcloud.com/bertpetkau

Hope Nuggets

Hope enables sorrow and grief to mend a broken heart.

CHAPTER FIFTEEN

BRIAN'S TRIBUTE

CELEBRATING BERT PETKAU (1955-2014)
– read at Bert's memorial

"*When I first met Bert, I was leading a Saturday-night church in downtown Mission. You just never knew what may happen. Who may walk through the doors. What challenges may occur or what remarkable may transpire.*

One evening something remarkable did happen.

When he walked through the doors, he didn't appear that "impressive" on the first look. To be honest, I thought it "may be one of those nights" ... Yet, what was really unusual was how he stood at the front of the church with a huge grin, and glowing with such joy as he watched the worship team ...

Months earlier, a mutual friend was telling me I had to meet this "kingdom" guy. I had heard so much about Bert Petkau, it was as if I knew him already, yet I didn't even know what he looked like.

Bert came to our Saturday-night Mission church that evening on a "whim" with a friend. What can I say – it was a very interesting evening. As we all know, Bert loved to worship and was also a passionate worship leader – the reason for the huge smile and gleaming face as he observed the worship team that evening.

So began a rich and full chapter of our lives for Kristen and I, as we developed a relationship and did life with Bert and Teresa.

Those of you who know Bert know what I mean when I say, "Bert didn't appear that impressive on the first look." Trying to impress or pizzazz anyone wasn't something that drove Bert – worship, composing, creating, loving and celebrating were the outflow of Bert's life. He loved and worshipped God and celebrated people in every walk of life.

Bert was one of the most generous people I know; I am sure you would agree. Bert and Teresa poured out into many people, churches, and ministries. Again, no interest in wanting to impress anyone – not having the left hand know what the right was doing was done naturally – though so much supernatural activity transpired in and around Bert's life.

One evening when one of our young leaders was passionately sharing. She was saying, "I have a God that is so BIG" – and in a heartbeat, Bert started formulating lyrics and composing music. The song "**I Have a Dream**" was birthed.

Bert moved in this dimension constantly, composing music and writing lyrics spontaneously, so in touch with his gifting while being led by the Holy Spirit.

"I have a dream that is so big, I have a strong desire. I have a vision in my heart, it is taking me so much higher." – The opening lyrics of "**I Have a Dream**."

This is signature Bert. Big dreams. A vision that encompassed and gathered so many others. You and me. Creative people. Pastors and leaders. Homemakers and builders. The least of these. No limits; everyone was included.

It not only took Bert higher – but all of us.

Yet his dream was so much larger. Dream City was birthed. Albums were developed.

Concerts and worship events. Through business, Bert and Teresa funded these Godly initiatives.

I have had the honour to spend time with Bert as he processed ideas, concepts and dreams. Things were always stirring and percolating within him. I will forever cherish those moments.

Bert tapped into the most unreached place on the planet: his own heart. The place God dwells within us. Where dreams are birthed and stirred.

The truth is, you can go to the most unreached places on the planet and preach the Gospel while never reaching into your own heart – in my opinion, the most unreached place on the Earth. Bert did that. He lived this and manifested it with passion.

Don't get me wrong. Bert and Teresa funded and supported missions, went on missions trips, and believed in reaching the world for Jesus.

Yet, Bert also had the courage and was fearless to reach into that place in his heart that can so often be the most scary – fear of failure is so nasty.

And yes, Bert had some failures. That is all part of our lives. It is reality. Although Bert just jumped back on the horse and rode again and again and again.

I know Bert would want me to say to you today: Go for it! Dream, develop a vision, trust God, and be open to unique ways that can fund your dreams. Don't be afraid to fail. It may hurt – you may go through a period of disillusionment and pain – but don't stay there. Get up and go again.

"The devil won't take me down 'cause I am on fire. I have a God that is so big, He is everything that I require." Bert's lyrics from **"I Have a Dream"** ... God is so big and everything you require ....Bert would want me to remind you not to let the devil or anyone steal your dreams.

Bert also created and invented in the construction industry. Always dreaming, always visioning.

Bert was a purist. He preferred being original. He didn't go with the flow, or I don't think he knew how to – you know what I mean?

Bert loved to ski, but only in fresh powder – not the groomed runs where most people skied.

Bert felt compelled to be an instrument to bring unity in our city.

Bert was crazy about his wife and would go to no limits to please her.

He loved his family and would talk often of his love for his kids.

His son Michael wrote this about his dad and posted it on Facebook:

"Even in his final two dark months on this planet, he showed no fear and remained content and happy with whatever the outcome might be. He was a good man. He gave me something to aspire to be and I was proud to call him my father."

So well said, Michael.

Thank you, Bert. You have inspired us and always will. Even facing death, you were fearless, content and happy. Like Michael, we are all so proud of you."

– Brian Olynick

Krysten Olynick

Sometimes, the Holy Spirit brings a couple into your lives who surround you with love and support and root for you endlessly. Brian and Kristen Olynick (K.O.) have shared life with our family since 2008. Bert and I had the privilege of climbing Mount Cheam in Chilliwack with them one magnificent summer day, and around 2009 we were honoured to have this couple baptize our oldest son, Christopher.

They were constant in prayer and helping with practical things during the late stages of Bert's cancer. Kristen was one of the few people with whom I shared my despair, sitting with me in those days of pain and heavy loss for us both. She gently loved me with her big brown eyes and comforted me through those trying times.

She is a woman who has stayed constant with me as a true friend. I love sharing life with her tenacious smile and vibrant love for life.

When we did church community those eight or so years ago, I remember her preaching a word that was electrifying. I actually wrote a poem back then about the message, and the impact it had on me that night. Again, thank you for always having my back, K.O.

Dynamic

She walks across the platform with authority
Her petite frame stunning,
Confident in Christ's love, held with integrity.
A woman commanding influence from above
Her eyes are like amber radiating fire from heaven
She speaks as a daughter of the Most High.
Like a warrior princess her hands are
prepared for war – her fingers to fight.
The scroll from her lips unravel
His words of truth.
She is explosive, astounding, and dynamite.

By Teresa Petkau

W.M.G.

With my God I can scale a wall
With my God I can run through a troop
With my God I can push back defenses
With my God I am not afraid
With my God I will not be shaken – No.

I will not be moved.
No one can hold me back.
No one can put me down
You are my stronghold. You are all I need
No one can take me away from your great love
Away from your great love

With my God we can run on the wall
With my God we can rush on the city
With my God we can push back defenses
With my God I am not afraid
With my God I will not be shaken – No.

I will not be moved.
Oh, oh, there's nothing anyone can do that
Could turn me away from you
Oh, Oh, there's nothing anyone could say
'Cause I know you're the only way
You are the strength of my heart.

Bert Petkau, *Dream*, 2011
https://soundcloud.com/bertpetkau

Hope Nuggets

Hope believes the cries of our hearts are heard in heaven.

CHAPTER SIXTEEN

THE MOURNING AFTER

I awoke the morning after the memorial and numbly walked downstairs. I felt I had aged ten years since September 20. But then, my jaw dropped as I saw what looked like a florist shop where our house used to be. Beautiful arrangements seemed to take up every inch surrounding the main floor. They had been delivered the night before while I slept.

I was not ready to read the dozens of notes and cards, yet so appreciated the love and kindness of everyone who reached out.

I sat down on the couch where I gazed each morning upon the beautiful valley below, and spent time with my Saviour. But this morning reality jolted me: My husband was gone. I told God how frightened I was and asked: "What is going to happen to my children and me?"

I could hear my daughter crying upstairs in her bedroom. My heart broke. I grasped my Bible and said to Him, "I love you. I know you are real." I implored Him to show me a word – any sign that He was with me so I could carry on. I opened the book, looking for something to help me believe Him in this tragedy and to help each of us survive even just this day.

God is faithful, and I was amazed when I opened my Bible to the following: *For I know the plans I have for you, declares the Lord, plans for welfare and not for evil, to give you a future and a hope." (Jeremiah 29:11)*

Those words resonated within my spirit. I whispered aloud, "Really? You do have a plan! There is hope, just as I asked!"

I got up and walked slowly upstairs to Summer's room. I crawled into bed and wrapped my arms around her. I said to her, "Summy, we both have holes in our hearts right now. But I want you to know that God does have a plan and a purpose for us."

She quietly nodded. With misty eyes, we lay there hoping that everything would somehow be okay. I sensed a trickle of the Father's peace begin to touch my soul.

But still, I wondered: How would this tragedy impact my children? How could they cope if I couldn't? There were no words to express the sorrow and grief we felt. A loving husband and father had been taken from us too soon and so quickly. I felt "ripped off," like an injustice had been done.

Mothers know that something supernatural takes place in birth. Pain gives way to the joy of new life, and instantly there is an unbreakable bond with her newborn child. The mother heart in me wanted to gather my chicks and say, "It's going to be all right." I wasn't responsible for what had happened to Bert – but I was responsible going forward. I thought I had to be the strong one. I didn't want my children to hurt. Somehow, in my own loss, I felt I needed to shoulder their pain as well. However, it didn't take long for me to realize that it was okay to accept my broken state and not have to be strong for everyone.

This was a faith-threatening turn in my life's journey. I felt like a part of me was missing, like someone had severed a limb. At my worst, I felt like I had been lopped in two. My Bert and I were truly one since that November day we wed in 1987.

The reality was, he was gone. I was missing my other half, and my children were missing their father.

Hope Nuggets

Hope is an assurance we are never left feeling alone.

CHAPTER SEVENTEEN

FROM MICHAEL

Michael's Dedication to His Father – November 22, 2014

Six days ago, the old man sitting in that chair lost his short, two-month battle with cancer. He left a great legacy behind. He accomplished things in his life that I cannot imagine accomplishing. Everything he did, he did out of sheer passion. Even with all his success, he seemed to possess a selflessness that it seems most people lose when they reach the heights he did. Even in his final two, dark months on this planet, he showed no fear, and remained content and happy with whatever the outcome might be.

He was a good man. He gave me something to aspire to be, and I was proud to call him my father.

Rest in peace, Dad.

The Petkau clan renting bikes at Stanley Park, Vancouver: Michael, Summer, Christopher, Sarah, Teresa and Bert.

CHAPTER EIGHTEEN

HOLDING ME UP

When my world was turned upside down, I would go to church and barely get through the worship times. I knew I needed to be there to soak in the presence of God, and to allow the Holy Spirit to soothe my pain. I knew I needed to be around people and avoid isolating myself.

My friends John and Diane Van Vloten faithfully surrounded me with love. They would stand on either side of me, like the pillars Aaron and Hur supporting weary Moses: When he was worn out, they responded by holding up his arms until the Israelites defeated the Amalekites in battle. *(Exodus 17:11)*

Diane, with tears in her eyes, would hold my hand throughout the worship, when the lyrics were too hard for me to sing. The words would touch a nerve in my heart, and at times cause me to crumble.

Being married to a worship leader for 27 years, I loved to worship God! I would focus and get lost in His presence. Somehow, the songs and music were in my DNA, and being in the very presence of the most high God touched me deeply.

Now it was different. John would put a protective, comforting arm around me, giving me the strength to get through each of those difficult Sunday services. I felt safe with these two friends, and it was nice not to sit alone. There were days I could only handle the music, and then I had to leave to go home and sleep. As weeks passed, I eventually could stay for the sermons.

How You Made the Stars

My heart is weak and I feel like crying
The joy within is very faint
The skies are grey and the sun isn't shining
But then you come when you hear me praying

But when I think of how you made the stars
I realize because of who you are
That you could heal my heart, Yeah

The number of sands in the seas and the length of my days
(Yes) And I'm beginning to see
How you made the stars
True peace within is what I'm seein'
True love again is what I feel
'Cause when you're near, I can't stop crying

These tears of joy, they flood my soul
'Cause you know my hopes and my dreams, and You know
my ways
The number of sands in the seas and the length of my days
It isn't hard to believe (in you) and I'm beginning to see
The truth (Yes),
And I'm beginning to see
How you made the stars.

Bert Petkau, *How You Made the Stars*, January 2009

"Come to me, all who labour and are heavy laden, and I will give you rest. Take my yoke upon you, and learn from me, for I am gentle and lowly in heart, and you will find rest for your souls. For my yoke is easy, and my burden is light" (Matthew 11: 28-30 ESV).

Hope Nuggets

Hope is a shield surrounding you with peace.

CHAPTER NINETEEN

HANGING ON

I was desperate for an angel's wing to cover me as my new journey unfolded. The evolution began, of learning how to survive after Bert's passing, and begin a new life on my own. The ups and downs of sorrow, grief and despair slammed me in waves. Nothing could take away the pain; my heart literally hurt.

In my devotions one morning, I came across a scripture I thought would never apply to me, but now it does. *Father of the fatherless and protector of widows is God in his holy habitation. (Psalm 68:5)*

In another verse it says, *He upholds the widow and the fatherless. (Psalm 146:9)*

I realized that I was a widow, and my children did not have their dad. This scripture became a source of strength over the coming months, as I watched how God truly protected me through every decision I had to make. In business or personal choices, no matter how overwhelming, He upheld our family and me.

I am always grateful for His sovereign love.

God does not allow suffering and pain to continue in the same way if we willingly fall into His loving arms. I made a choice that November morning. I could crawl into my bed and die of a broken heart, or call out to God to help me take baby steps and get through each day. I clung to his words of *a hope* and *a future* for me – and that God had allowed this to happen. I was convinced that somehow He was working in the midst of it all, and the fragments of my brokenness would be pieced back together.

After all, He is God, and I believe He is all-knowing. My relationship with Him is real. I asked Him for strength to help me live, and for peace to carry on – and my loving and caring God gave me exactly that! Afternoon naps helped me cope, and when my head hit the pillow at night I was fast asleep. It was probably from emotional exhaustion; more tiring than any physical trial.

A few weeks later was our company Christmas party. I knew our employees would be wondering how I was doing, so I was determined to attend – until I had a meltdown that morning. I was sitting on my bedroom floor bawling my eyes out. Chris and Sarah were making breakfast in the kitchen and heard me crying upstairs. They both came up to me, and I'll never forget how Sarah sweetly came over, wrapped her arms around me and held tight. My son said, "Mom, you're going to be okay, and we are here for you."

They helped me work through my emotions, and I pulled myself together. We went as a family to the Christmas party, and I again asked God for strength to help me be a light that evening. In my fragile state, I bravely faced those who loved Bert. Our oldest son, Chris, honoured his dad with a few special words, and I put my arm around Bert's business partner, Ruben, as he paid tribute with tears in his eyes. All of us missed our leader.

It was a difficult night, but the kids and I got through without another meltdown.

God in Heaven

There's a light in the darkness
There's a hope. There's a love
That's burning deep inside.
There's a place I have found
Where mercy still abounds
And grace is there to find.
Lord of all the heavens of all the universe
The greatness of your love I can't understand.
God of all creation Maker of my heart
Lead me to your presence once again
God in Heaven.
There's a passion. There's a hope.
A cry in every heart
That's calling out for you
There's a love, there's a joy
There's a peace that's greater
And grace is there to find.
I can find you
'Cause your love grows ever stronger
I will seek you Lord
Here in your presence
God in Heaven.

Bert Petkau, *How You Made the Stars*, January 2002

Rahab

I think of so many Biblical stories where God unexpectedly used someone in his story that didn't look like they had much going for them. Rahab, the prostitute from Jericho, hid the spies when they were sent to prepare the way for Joshua to take the city. She took them to the top of the roof and concealed them under stalks of flax she had laid out.

She knew the two spies were men of God, servants of the most high, and she hid them so that her life would be spared. Ultimately, she married Salmon of the tribe of Judah and was the mother of Boaz, the husband of Ruth (Joshua 2:1-23; Matthew 1:5).

God became Rahab's kinsman redeemer. His covenant with Israel foreshadows the redemption of humanity through Jesus Christ's sacrifice for us on the cross. Rahab received God's mercy. He chose to spare a prostitute and include her in the lineage of Jesus.

Wow! Pretty cool. She was a heroine of the faith, and the Biblical writers told her story. God uses the weak in the world – those who are humble – to complete His plan and purposes. He chose one of the least likely to be a part of the lineage of our Saviour Jesus Christ. (See Joshua Chapter 2)

CHAPTER TWENTY

MY DAD'S DREAM

By Chris Petkau

My dad, Bert Petkau, taught me a lot of things growing up. He taught me how to ride a bike, how to swing a hammer, and he tried to teach me the guitar, which to this day I wish I had stuck with. But one thing he taught me, whether it was on purpose or not, was to dream.

I remember having many conversations with him about the church, music, art, and God, discussing song ideas, movie ideas, and new and creative ways to show people who God was. He felt like God wanted to do something big in the Christian music industry, but couldn't quite put his finger on what it exactly was – and so Dream City was born.

Dream City is based on this scripture:

By faith Abraham, when he was called, obeyed by going out to a place which he was to receive for an inheritance; and he went out, not knowing where he was going. By faith he lived as an alien in the land of promise, as in a foreign land, dwelling in tents with Isaac and Jacob, fellow heirs of the same promise; for he was looking for the city which has foundations, whose architect and builder is God. (Hebrews 11:8-10)

Since he started his journey, a lot of the vision has come into focus. My dad believed music, art and media could be used to unite the church, reach the lost, and glorify Jesus Christ. Those three I remember, were his biggest priorities. Talking with him, if we weren't talking about one of those topics, then what the heck were we talking about? And I fully agreed.

Bert Petkau passed away of colon and liver cancer in November of 2014, with his dream feeling more real than the day it was conceived in his heart. He passed away still believing, like Abraham, that although he had not seen the fulfillment of his promise, it would surely come to pass.

I, Chris Petkau; my wife, Sarah; Dad's wife and my mother, Teresa Petkau; and many others are dedicated to continuing the dream of my father and believe, like he believed, that this is bigger than one man or one ministry.

Thanks for checking out my dad's music and believing in Dream City with us.

It is my desire that we would take what is resonating within us and release it upon the Earth. **Lights & Ocean** *is just a small part of a big vision that is stirring. I pray that this vision would be released in our hearts, in this city, and on the earth.*

Listening to **Seven Songs**, *the things of earth crumble away, making room for Heaven to become the burning reality of your heart. The songs provide hope and promise for those facing the crowding pressures of this world.*

Our hearts can be free when Heaven reigns in them. The experience of His love can give us assurance that one day our faith will become sight. 'Seven Songs' welcomes you to experience this joy, and live for a world and a King more real than what your eyes see.

Downloads of these albums are at:
https://soundcloud.com/bertpetkau

Let Your Glory Fall

Let your glory fall upon us as we praise you
Let your presence rest among us as we worship you
Let the anointing of Your Spirit fill our hearts with praise
As we worship the King.
Hallelujah, we worship the King
Hallelujah, we worship the King
Hallelujah, we worship the King
Hallelujah, we worship the King.

Bert Petkau, *Soldier Boy*, 1998

Hope Nuggets

Hope is the dream in our hearts moving us forward with expectancy.

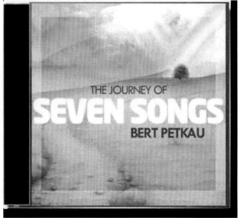

CHAPTER TWENTY-ONE

A FIRST CHRISTMAS "WITHOUT"

My children got up one morning in December and suggested we get out of the house – try to do something fun as a family. They wanted to go cut a real, live Christmas tree, so we decided to do it.

We borrowed the family truck of Summer's best friend, hoping to find the perfect tree for the 21-foot ceiling in our great room. Petite little Rachel was driving for Summer while my boys and nephew Andy came with me.

I was still in a relative fog, but remember it as a crisp, sunny day. We walked high up a hill at the tree farm, looking past the Charlie Brown versions and scanning rows for the perfect specimen. We agreed on a stately pine, and my nephew chain-sawed it to haul it back to the truck. There was no one else around, so we phoned the posted number to see where to pay. Nobody answered, so the tree was wrapped and loaded, and I planned to come back the next day to settle up.

The boys got the conifer into the house and steadied it into the stand. The smell was delightful! The girls offered to do the decorating, so I went upstairs for a much-needed nap. A couple of hours later, I came downstairs to a beautifully adorned Christmas tree! It actually looked stunning against the big, glass door with the blue sky behind it.

The next day, I went back to pay. It was Saturday, so lots

of families were out to play Paul Bunyan. I found the owner and told him we had come the day before, but no one had been around. I figured I owed 90 or 100 dollars for a tree that big.

He looked at me in disbelief; shocked that I actually returned, and said: "Just give me $20 and enjoy your tree." The smile on my face belied the sorrow in my heart, and I looked to heaven and said, "Thank you."

A couple of weeks later it was nearly Christmas. I wrote a card to Bert's parents and made them a copy of the CD about Bert's life that we had shown at the memorial service. His parents live in Ontario, so I stopped by Shoppers Drug Mart to mail the package.

When I came out to my vehicle, I noticed not one, but two flat tires on the driver's side. Stunned, I instinctively picked up my phone to call Bert for help.

I knew instantly my mistake. I sat helplessly in the car with tears streaming down. This may seem odd, but it was too draining for me to call someone else. The rims could wreck if I drove on flats, but I didn't know what else to do. So, I took a chance and slowly drove to the nearest tire shop where they fixed one tire and replaced the other. Thankfully, the rims survived.

That day was a surreal epiphany. I was abruptly reminded that my flesh-and-blood protector no longer had my back. I was learning a sense of self-reliance, and, far more importantly, to rely more than ever on Abba; Father God. I was trusting Him for strength, independence, and being my safety net now that Bert was gone.

It was God's mercy that carried my family and me through our first Christmas without Bert. We lit a candle that stood by his photo, and just went through the motions that day.

Then New Year's Day came and went in what was, to me, a cloudy haze. Still, we discovered as a family, we did quite well pulling together. They say holidays are stressful even in the best of times, so we were proud to navigate ours without a shipwreck or breakdown. I even felt well enough in January to read through the bag of cards and notes expressing love and condolences to the Petkau family.

Over the holiday season, the realization hit us that the year about to unfold would be full of new beginnings.

Do Not Be Overwhelmed

Fear not, for I have redeemed you; O Israel:
I have called you by name, you are mine.
When you pass through the waters, I will be with you;
And through the rivers, they shall not overwhelm you;
When you walk through fire you shall not be burned,
And the flame shall not consume you.
Because you are precious in my eyes, and honoured,
and I love you.
(Isaiah 42: 1, 2, 4)

Hope Nuggets

Hope is a constant in an uncertain world.

CHAPTER TWENTY-TWO

LIKE GIDEON

My family and I were adjusting to the new year in January, trying to live a day at a time and coping with whatever was ahead for each of us. I was now dealing with the central banks; two different businesses; what to do with my husband's insurance, investments, government documents, and the things he had invented for the construction industry – the list seemed to grow with each passing month.

My mind was boggled, and I was not prepared for all this. After all, I was Bert's wife and supporter – not the creative and brilliant business person he was gifted to be. It would have been a breeze for him to deal with all the business stuff.

At one point, it was so overwhelming that I wanted to hide under the covers and not come out. I was not only dealing with my own pain, but also with concern for my kids' welfare. My heart was shattered and my head hurt.

I remember the day I went to the bank for the first time. My friend Peter came along, but I was so dazed, I felt like a little lamb going off to slaughter. If Peter not been with me, I probably would have given everything away.

I also needed help around the house. Door handles were broken, the washing machine leaked, something was stuck in the dishwasher under the heating element, my patio fire table had a dangerous gas leak, and I couldn't program my air conditioner.

The temptation to feel sorry for myself was very real.

It's easy to be thankful when life is treating you well, but it's a different story when life hits you with difficulties. In order to fight against discouragement, I prayed, practised thankfulness, took a deep breath, and trusted each day that my handyman issues would somehow get resolved.

No matter how I was feeling, there were issues that had to be dealt with in those early months. To my amazement, different people came to my aid, and every single challenge was addressed. What's more, none of the guys would let me pay them! I was astonished.

I was grateful God put the right people into my life to help me cope with those overwhelming, unexpected tasks. I was forced to take baby steps – tiny mustard seeds of faith. There were days I could hardly hear or discern the voice of God, and it all seemed too much to bear. I felt like Gideon in the Bible,

"Pardon me, my lord," Gideon replied, "but if the Lord is with us, why has all this happened to us? Where are all his wonders that our ancestors told us about when they said, Did not the Lord bring us up out of Egypt? But now the Lord has abandoned us and given us into the hand of Midian."

The Lord turned to him and said, "Go in the strength you have and save Israel out of Midian's hand. Am I not sending you?"

"Pardon me, my lord," Gideon replied, "but how can I save Israel? My clan is the weakest in Manasseh, and I am the least in my family."

The Lord answered, "I will be with you, and you will strike down all the Midianites, leaving none alive."

Gideon replied, "If now I have found favour in your eyes, give me a sign that it is really you talking to me. (Judges 6:13-17)

This passage reminded me of me. The Lord came through that first day of my brokenness, and gave me a promise of hope and a future for us as a family. Poor Gideon – I surely could relate to him. Somehow, in my weakness, I was learning to surrender. And by taking those tiny steps of faith, my God was faithful not to leave me in a bind.

When Gideon realized God's favour was with him, and he mustered up the strength, courage, and wisdom to listen to the Lord. He defeated the Midianites, and there were 40 years of peace during Gideon's lifetime. God was helping me trust him for the same ability to overcome.

Hope Nuggets

Bravery is Hope that never gives up.

God in Heaven

There's a light in the darkness
There's a hope. There's a love
That's burning deep inside.
There's a place I have found
Where mercy still abounds
And grace is there to find.
Lord of all the heavens of all the universe
The greatness of your love I can't understand.
God of all creation Maker of my heart
Lead me to your presence once again
God in Heaven.
There's a passion. There's a hope.
A cry in every heart
That's calling out for you
There's a love, there's a joy
There's a peace that's greater
And grace is there to find.
I can find you
Cause your love grows ever stronger
I will seek you Lord
Here in your presence
God in Heaven.

Bert Petkau, *How You Made the Stars*, January 2002.

Hope Nuggets

Hope is a grace path, new every day, filled with
thankfulness.

CHAPTER TWENTY-THREE

BLESSED BY GRACE

As God continued to show his grace on my life – his unconditional love and undeserved favour – I was learning how to show that same kind of grace to others around me in a new way.

A powerful scripture that has helped me process this idea is found in Corinthians:

But He said to me, My grace (My favour and loving-kindness and mercy) is enough for you [sufficient against any danger and enables you to bear the trouble manfully]; for My strength and power are made perfect (fulfilled and completed) and show themselves most effective in [your] weakness. Therefore, I will all the more gladly glory in my weaknesses and infirmities, that the strength and power of Christ (the Messiah) may rest (yes, may pitch a tent over and dwell) upon me! (II Corinthians 12:9 AMP)

This tells me that, among other things, God's grace is available to help me in difficult circumstances when I choose it, and grace can give me the power to be gracious to others when naturally it would be hard.

In the first months after Bert, whenever I was out, there were some people who recognized me and awkwardly came up to give me a hug. They and others offered kind condolences.

Some others would stand in shock and cry, doing their best to be strong. Some of them were in disbelief and apologized for crying. I responded by saying, "It's okay. I truly understand."

In my thoughts, I knew that Jesus understood what I was going through, and how hard these encounters were for me in the moment. He really did know, not just because He is all-knowing, but because of His own experiences with suffering. God was giving me the grace to see that people really were concerned about me and that they were also grieving the loss of someone they admired and loved in their own way.

I remember it was raining when a musician friend of Bert's came into the grocery store as I was going out. He recognized me and gave me a hug, expressing how he could not believe that Bert was gone. I let him mourn for his friend, and we both had tears in our eyes.

Over the months, people were encouraging and kind, and I'm grateful for all the prayers, caring words, and messages for my family. I also encountered some difficult reactions, but something inside reminded me to think of grace when negative words were spoken. I belong to Jesus, and He is building a strength in me. He reminds me: Our destiny is determined by Him, not people, so I kept my heart still. There will always be people who don't understand.

My girlfriend Jacqueline was with me one time when we met a lady who had heard the sad news. She casually asked, "So how are you doing, being a widow?" I could hardly believe it, and Jacqueline was stunned. How do you answer that? "It sucks" is what I thought to say, but decided to be gracious and responded, "I'm healing and living one day at a time."

In another encounter, I met someone whose first words after greeting were, "How long are you going to stay in that big house of yours?" How she knew the size of my house was a surprise, as she had never been there.

Again I responded, "I'm healing and living one day at a time."

My "grace learning curve" did not make it easier to have lost Bert, but I was slowly coming to understand a new type of kindness and patience with people. I realized, most were well-meaning and trying to relate, and death is awkward to talk about. Grace keeps us tender in those uncomfortable moments.

Bert once looked up the word "meekness" – it means controlled strength. I would think of that when I ran into people, and when, for months, I received Bert's work emails from people who had no idea he was gone.

With controlled strength I acknowledged each inquiry and managed each situation, letting them know he had passed away, and asking them how I could be of assistance.

I saw God's grace in my new journey without Bert, and how He was so gracious to look after me and uphold me each day. He did not leave me floundering.

Grace is represented by the number five. Each of my three children has the number five in the calendar year of their birthday and we were a family of five. Yes, I'm grateful we were and are a family of His grace.

Amazing Grace

What can I offer You, give You in return
This desolate heart undone
You shed your blood, You died for me
God's perfect wondrous son.

Humility poured out upon a cross
Love staggering through unclouded hope.

Unmerited favour for all of mankind
Repaid debts for you and me.

Crimson red, blood-stained love
Healing mercy sets us free.

On my knees in sweet surrender
Hands open mercy received
Eyes heaven bound, You chose me
This is truly amazing grace.

By Teresa Petkau

Hope Nuggets

Hope is small victories attained by constant prayer.

CHAPTER TWENTY-FOUR

MY ANGELS SOFTEN THE BLOW

I am so grateful for my girlfriends who took time to go out for coffee with me in those early days. I'm very thankful they did not try to "fix" me, but let me reminisce about life with Bert. I soaked a lot of Kleenex and coffee shop napkins while they held my hand.

It felt good to release slivers of pain and heartache. We were all grieving in our own ways, perhaps still wishing to deny this had really taken place.

"Girlfriend" is inaccurate for the vital role these loving, supportive friends played: Jacqueline Harrison, Kristine Olynick, April Bartsch, Sandy Thiessen, Michele Cartwright, Joyce Grubb, Trish Ratzlaff, Lisa and David Lowndes, Jennifer Brown, and Joy Perry. Each of them was a pillar.

April Klassen, a young woman who had recently lost her mother to cancer, sought me out a month after Bert had gone. She truly was my little angel who understood exactly what I was going through.

Through the grieving process, there were times I needed the faith of others to carry me. Looking back now with a clearer frame of mind, I am so thankful for everyone who reached out to me. God brought them into my life to steady my heart and help me inch forward.

In private, I also gave myself permission to release how I

was feeling, good or bad, rather than internalizing it. Countless tears brought release. Journaling my thoughts and sometimes writing notes to God helped with my confusion and fear. I learned that as I surrendered to my pain, and as I surrendered to Him, He began my healing process.

A little later in spring, friends Joyce and Michele joined in on what was, for me right then, a big step out of that fear. A year previously, Bert and I had attended an Abbotsford fundraiser and won a week at a three-bedroom condo in Palm Springs, California. We had planned to use it this year, but now, without Bert, and with my kids unable to join me for various reasons, I texted these two and invited them along. Amazingly, within fifteen minutes both their husbands were on board for Michele and Joyce to venture off with me!

I used air miles to book a ticket out of Abby, and mustered up the courage to fly and meet two of my "besties." It was the first time I had flown on my own since I was single in my 20s. It was intimidating, with what I'd been through, but I needed a break from the turbulence.

We rented a car and Michele served as my GPS girl. (I'm sometimes "navigationally challenged" – without my iPhone GPS, I don't know where I would end up.) We went to Costco for groceries and decided to eat out every other day. The condo was beautiful, with a lovely backyard pool. The weather was hot, but not unbearable.

I loved pajama parties when I was a young girl. We would stay up all hours doing crazy things like having pillow fights, jumping on the bed, watching movies, eating popcorn and, of course, talking about the boys we liked at school. Now there are no pillow fights, but Michele, Joyce and I enjoyed this extended time together, hanging out as friends.

We would awake in the mornings to me reading my devotional book by Sarah Young, then pray together. Joyce was a fabulous cook and made amazing dinners. We relaxed by the pool, sharing life and, of course, Michele knew where all the good shopping spots were.

I heard long ago that if you have been blessed with one good friend, you are truly blessed. All the women God put into my life are so amazing, and I am so grateful for these two. The trip was the breath of oxygen that I needed just then. I realized while I was waiting for my connecting flight home that I had begun to laugh again!

I expected my daughter to pick me up at the Abby airport. To my surprise, Summy arrived with Chris and Sarah, who handed me a bouquet of red roses – just a few hours late for Mother's Day. Chris brought me an Earl Grey tea latte, exactly the way I like. My heart danced.

Thank you, Papa God, I am so blessed.

Hope Nuggets

Hope is a flower budding into a fragrant rose.

CHAPTER TWENTY-FIVE

HIS EYE IS ON THE SPARROW

One Sunday morning, back at the end of December, another friend checked up on me during a coffee break at church. Vi Wiens had been facilitating a Bible study at a treatment centre nearby and asked me if I would like to get involved. I told her I would pray about it and get back to her.

Two months later, I was thinking about Vi and decided to meet up with her to learn more. She told me the Bible study was for women who had been through a lot in their lives and had a desire to break free from various addictions. Some had been in jail, and most of them have very young children.

When she first approached me, Vi said she had been praying and the Lord clearly put me on her heart. She felt that my gifts would be an asset to these women in their recovery. So, I decided to check it out.

I understood the truth that taking my eyes off of myself and giving to someone else would be good for me. So I felt it was right to volunteer if someone could be blessed through my contribution. And if healing came my way because of it, so much the better.

I was amazed by these women and their first-time questions, hungry to know who the God of the Bible is, and why He loves them. Many of them had never been in church, and to some of them, God was whatever you wanted Him to be.

The girls could choose between Bible study or another meeting on Tuesday nights. I remember one young woman who came to check us out. She was a young mother and appeared to be a tough chick with a real chip on her shoulder. But she was interested to hear about "the God stuff" because she wanted something for her young son.

As the weeks passed, I saw her countenance change slowly from hard to tender. Little by little, you could see the Holy Spirit working in her life. Eventually, with tears in her eyes, I had the privilege of leading her to Jesus Christ.

Over the months, many of the women became Christ followers, though I was saddened by one lady's reality. She had been in the program for three weeks and was hungry to know more about God. She was full of life and had quite the sense of humour. She was very candid about her situation and past struggles.

One night she bowed her head and asked Jesus Christ to come into her heart. When she finished praying, she let out a "Yahoo!" You could see that something powerful had transpired.

Three weeks later, she went home for a weekend visit, relapsed, and had to leave the program. I realized it was no accident that she had chosen to attend the program, even though at this point it looked like she had "failed." I believe God saw her heart the night she said "yes" to his forgiveness and mercy, and a seed of hope was planted in her.

Angie Janzen, Vi and I prayed together weekly before going to the group, asking God to lead and direct our steps. The three of us tag-teamed together to answer their questions, but also to remind them that life is a series of daily choices, and if we make good ones, they will bear sweet fruit.

We also had many praying for the three of us via email each week, and it was evident by the changes happening in each of these women's lives that prayers were being answered. I remember one very rainy night after we were done Angie and I stood outside in amazement at what the Holy Spirit was doing. We were like two giddy schoolgirls standing in the rain, praising God and thanking Him for this opportunity. We almost had to pinch ourselves, that we could be part of it.

As I got to know the ladies in the program, with new ones coming every week, I fell in love with each of them. I went with the attitude that we are all on a healing journey together, and it is a love relationship with Jesus Christ that we all need to encounter daily.

As I suspected it might, the Holy Spirit was using this not only to bring healing and freedom to these broken women, but also to begin the process of healing my heart! I was learning to have compassion like I never knew before.

Fast forward to a beautiful afternoon later in the year, when I went with some friends to the unique little town of Fort Langley – one of my favourite places to relax and enjoy the sunshine. We went into a popular little café for a bowl of chili and when it was my turn to order, the young woman across the counter said, "I know you!" Her face looked familiar as her eyes danced with joy.

It was one of the many young women I had come to know at the treatment centre months before. Tamara and I locked eyes with excitement, and she ran from behind the counter to give me a big hug! What a delight to see her doing so well, working with people in a job she loved while raising her young son. She was following her plan with the help of the Holy Spirit, living life a day at a time and successfully making good choices.

I was so proud of her and all she had accomplished and thrilled to have had a small part in her life. She was succeeding in overcoming her addiction and conquering the demons that once plagued her.

This little sparrow, like myself, was given a second chance, and the reality of God's love and destiny for her was evident. Seeing her thriving encouraged my heart tremendously, and gave me hope for my own future. There is truly something about giving of yourself that, in return, becomes a special blessing in your life.

Quiescent Rest

Early in the morning before dawn awakens
The sun in its brilliance peaks upon the horizon.
Birds chirp softly as creation stirs.
The smell of purple lilacs linger
Tall grasses sway in the morning breeze.
The quiet hush of the wind rustles over the valley
God's peace rests upon the land.
In quiescent rest tranquility soothes the heart of man.
The hand of God slips His love over each vessel.
A duvet of gentleness wraps its calm over heartache
The solace of love whispers assurance to a healing soul.

By Teresa Petkau

Hope Nuggets

Hope opens the door of our hearts to reach out
to the vulnerable.

CHAPTER TWENTY-SIX

HE CRUSHES OVER US

Michael lives in Vancouver, and Chris and Sarah got back from Campbell River in March, after Chris was working on our construction job there. Summer was living with me, and I felt it was important that we walked our journeys of healing together after Bert's death. So, once a month we got together for supper.

Young people and their schedules can be challenging, but we succeeded in gathering every four weeks for a meal. The kids would come over to my place, and we would hang out and connect. It was so nice to hear the laughter in the background as I worked preparing dinner. The kids engaged in small talk or conversations in depth. We didn't realize it, but they were supporting each other as well as me.

We are a somewhat independent bunch, and what I experienced was a family growing closer in a way we had never known. When we united, the kids reminisced about their dad – things they thought were funny about Bert, what he taught them about their struggles, and how to overcome and cope with life.

It was a special time of connecting as a family. As a mom, I was concerned about doing my best to support each of them in what they faced. Loss is difficult, but through the trauma, we were pulling together. I was so proud of my children –

and their father would also have been proud – as the first year without him unfolded for each of us.

When I look at my children, I see the miracle of both Bert and me in them. Christopher is intensely deep, loyal and creative. He's a young man who is incredibly gifted with lyrics (just like his dad) and has a heart for music; mostly rap or hip-hop.

Michael, a thinker and deeply creative, wrote amazing stories when he was young. He loved to watch films and gather ideas for movies and screenplays. One day I hope he will have a desire to use this gift again. I think he looks exactly like his dad, and people often comment on how much he resembles Bert.

Summer, our "little girl", has a strength that calls for social justice in the world! What's more, she is beautiful, sensible, has a great sense of humour, and is so good with people.

I know that Bert is cheering us all on. The love he shared, and the reflection of who he was, will forever live within our children – and perhaps our grandchildren one day.

As I think of the healing process for us as a family, I am so proud of the strength and courage my children possess. I pray for them daily, and I know that God has their best interests in mind.

I think of how much I love my kids and how much God loves them as well. The word "crush" pops into my mind, like when you have a crush on someone in high school. I was thinking of God and how He "crushes" over each one of us! We are special, and He holds each one of us close to His heart.

His Love Is Over Me

I am weak – I am faint with love.
Strengthen me again, with your love.
Lead me near, lead me to your side,
To the one that my heart loves.

'Cause His love is over me.
His love is over me. His love is over me.
Your mercy, your love is ever over me.

Winter is past, the rains are gone,
Flowers do appear again.
The sounds of singing lead me along,
To the one that my heart loves.

'Cause His love is over me.
His love is over me. His love is over me.
Your mercy, your love is ever over me.
Your love is over me. Your love is over me.
Your mercy, your love is ever over me.

I am weak – I am faint with love.
Strengthen me again, with your love.
Lead me near, lead me to your side
To the one that my heart loves.

His love is over me.
His love is over me. His love is over me.
Your mercy, your love is ever over me.

Bert Petkau, *Seven Songs*, 2011.
https://soundcloud.com/bertpetkau

The Father Heart of God

He encircled him, he cared for him, he kept him as the apple
of his eye. Like an eagle that stirs up its nest, that flutters over
its young, spreading out its wings, catching them, bearing them
on its pinions, the Lord alone guided him.
(Deuteronomy 32:10-11 ESV)

Hope Nuggets

Hope is the love of family pulling together in difficult situations.

CHAPTER TWENTY-SEVEN

ANOTHER GOODBYE

Spring was around the corner, and I was living one day at a time. My heart was mending ever so slowly. My daughter and I were doing laundry and chatting away in the laundry room one day. She said, "Mom, I have some good news." It was the first time in months that I actually saw a smile on her face.

Summer had written a letter to Youth With a Mission (YWAM) in Kona, Hawaii, volunteering to work in their Mission Builders Program. She had been accepted to serve there, but they needed help soon. Summer had loved doing high school missions in Thailand and Costa Rica over spring breaks and she was excited to get involved again.

When she told me this, my heart briefly froze. I was happy for her, but I also realized I would be completely on my own. I didn't let my emotions show. I knew that God was in this. He would be with me again, helping me clear another hurdle.

I mentioned to Summer that she would have to pay her way, and if everything fell into place, we would know it was God's will for her to go. She put together her letter seeking financial support, emailing it to whomever God had put on her heart.

Within weeks, she received all she needed! I saw a bounce in her step; a hope and a future for her was unfolding. Thank you, Lord!

Sometimes, as parents, it's tough to let go of our children. I learned the hard way when my boys were in their teens, and we were facing some challenges with them. I was forced to let go, especially with my firstborn son, Chris.

Our children are on loan to us – they belong to God. I eventually realized it when I gave Chris to the care of our heavenly Father. He went off to Bible school – of all places, it was in South Carolina! As much as I hated to see him leave, it could have been much worse.

It was clearly what he wanted to do, and of course, I missed him. He was down in the American South for three years, coming home for summer to work in construction. Then, of all things, he fell in love with an American girl – not a Canadian!

The Holy Spirit surely knows what He is doing. His ways are so much higher than ours. I have a special love for Chris' wife Sarah. She is perfect for him and fits so well into our crazy family dynamics. She would call Bert "Dad," and they teased each other with their similar sense of humour.

"Letting go" brings a plan and purpose much better than what we might have first envisioned, and the end result seems so right because His ways are higher than ours. In my daughter's case, I knew in my heart this was something she needed to do and was an essential part of her healing journey, as much as I hated to see her go.

Behold, children are a heritage from the Lord,
the fruit of the womb a reward.
Like arrows in the hand of a warrior
are the children of one's youth.
Blessed is the man
who fills his quiver with them!
He shall not be put to shame
when he speaks with his enemies in the gate.
(Psalms 127:3-5)

Hadassah

What was it about this woman God pursued!
A young maiden of honour and grace.
Hadassah was destined for greatness,
A woman humble and wise, called upon by the most high God.

She set out to redeem her people, free them from despair.
God looked down and smiled.
He saw her courage, her tenacity, her love.
The king extended his sceptre her way.

The one above the King of kings bestowed His favour,
Beloved Ester stara, a Persian word for "star!"
She, a heroine, saved a nation from destruction.
You, my Sarah, patient and kind, bestowed love my way –
God's sceptre of love
Forever grateful you are a gift to this family.

By Teresa Petkau, lovingly for Sarah Petkau

Hope Nuggets

Hope is the assurance we are never left alone.

CHAPTER TWENTY-EIGHT

DAYS WITHOUT SUMMER

I had mixed emotions when I woke up that day in May, knowing my daughter was heading to Hawaii for 12 weeks. I was excited for her new adventure, and how God was going to use her and minister His healing love to her. Still, I knew it would be another adjustment.

We were driving to the Vancouver airport that morning. I had some business in the city, with a lawyer regarding company stuff, so I got an appointment on the day of her flight out.

Summer and I talked in the car about life and the excitement of wondering what was in store for her. We prayed together and trusted God for a safe flight and that I would be okay on my own.

My "little girl" – wearing her backward baseball cap, jeans and Converse runners – left her suitcase at the luggage drop. Then, with backpack in hand, she hugged me and we said our goodbyes. I typed the lawyer's address into my GPS, and off I went to downtown Vancouver.

The traffic took forever, and I seemed to hit every red light on the way (patience!). My phone dinged, and I noticed a text from Summer. After I found a parking spot on Burrard Street, I read it: She was stuck at YVR, telling me she would miss her connecting flight in San Francisco – and her luggage would fly to Kona without her.

I knew I couldn't help her this time. This was a Summer learning experience, but I knew God would be with her. It was quite the 24 hours for my girl. When she did get to San Francisco, she flew from there to Oahu and got up in the middle of the night to catch her flight to Kona. Then it was back and forth to the airport the next day trying to get her suitcase. I was relieved that night when she texted saying that her luggage had finally shown up.

For Summer, this stepping out was an unforgettable time, filled with adventure, joy, hard work, healing, and the making of treasured friendships. For me, it was another challenging step towards living life on my own.

The first three days of her absence were probably the most difficult I had to encounter in 2015. The eerie silence in my home without her was so hard to bear. My heart ached, and my mind was racing with anxiety – an uneasiness about being alone and uncertainty about my future.

Eventually, I did go out with friends, to gatherings where nearly everyone was married – anniversaries, birthday parties, and other events where it felt terribly awkward without my other half. I learned that it's possible to feel alone and isolated even in a roomful of people.

I remember thinking "no one understands what I'm going through" – adjusting to living alone and having no one to share my thoughts with. It seemed unfair having to sit in silence at home without my daughter to talk to. When I was young, it was okay to feel lonely at times, because the situation was so different. But this was hitting me hard, a double whammy of grief: the emptiness of two special people missing from my life.

Again I cried, and somehow I picked up the broken pieces of my life and handed them over to God.

You have kept count of my tossings, put my tears in your bottle. Are they not in your book? (Psalm 56:8)

God holds my tears in a bottle and counts each of them! Once again, I had to surrender it all, trusting that He understood, and felt my pain. He, the faithful one, is all knowing and does not leave his children suffering forever.

I found as I emptied my emotions in God's presence, my burden grew lighter. I was understood. I was not carrying grief on my own. My soul was being relieved, and I was learning more about the depth and breadth of who He really is.

He was my refuge and safe place, flooding my soul with unconditional love. As I released my sorrow, I realized that although I had suffered a staggering loss, it did not mean my life was over. We all go through situations we do not understand. In my valleys, I was learning that faith is trusting God in the dark places.

Some time after Summer left, God brought my daughter-in-law Sarah more closely into my life. She and Chris had just found a basement suite down the street from me – how cool was that! – and now Chris was away working in Campbell River for a couple of weeks.

During that time, Sarah and I would get together, often sharing about our journeys, and what we were learning through it all. God was piecing all our lives back together in His perfect timing. I got to know her on a personal level, not just as my son's wife. I learned who she really was and discovered the beautiful heart of patience and kindness that beat within her.

Sarah and I soon bonded in a way that was so precious. We would take her dog Nala, and Summer's pup Lucy, to the top of nearby Eagle Mountain and chat, where the warmth of the sun and the breeze brushed over our faces. In awe, we stared at beautiful Mount Baker in front of us. As her mother-in-law, I pinched myself that I got to share life with her. I love that little southern belle! The Holy Spirit knew I would have to make a huge adjustment while Summer was away and He brought Sarah to help me adapt.

When I eventually picked up my girl at the airport after her 12-week adventure in Kona, I was so thrilled to see a twinkle in her eye and enthusiasm from time well spent. All the way home, she shared amazing experiences from this chapter of her young life: friendships she would never forget; words of healing for her heart from those who didn't know of Bert's passing; hiking in the night to a volcano framed by blazing stars; waterfalls and dolphin pools.

This was a magical time that God knew her tender heart needed. In spite of my days without Summy, my heart was filled with joy knowing God had been teaching us both a new strength and courage, and showing us that He does have our best interests in mind. Somehow, having to be on my own, I felt God was preparing me for something through this experience; arranging for my future to bring hope to others and honour and glory to Him.

For He satisfies the longing soul and the hungry soul He fills with good things. His peace I rest in. (Psalm 107:9)

CHAPTER TWENTY-NINE

THROUGH YOUR EYES OF LOVE

May 21, 2015 6:45 a.m.

Bert would have really active dreams when he slept. He remembered many and took notes about them. But when I sleep at night, I rarely remember anything. So, this Thursday morning was a unique experience for me. I didn't know if I'd had a dream, a vision, or an encounter – but it was very real.

I woke up and looked at my clock, and I remember it reading 6:45. I thought to myself that I'd fall back to sleep for a few more minutes, then get up. When I closed my eyes, I clearly saw Bert as if he was right with me, in the basement of a house I didn't know. I remember thinking, "Oh, Bert's home from work." He was walking toward a shower with a white towel wrapped around him and was about to step into it. I said to him, "Oh, Honey, you're home from work."

He turned around and looked at me with such love! His blue eyes were glowing, and he looked really good and healthy. I walked to him, and he put his arms around me and held me close. I remember putting my nose against his cheek and taking a deep breath as I enjoyed his scent. I told him, "Honey, I really miss you."

Bert responded, "I love you." Then I woke up. It was so real and vivid – and I felt such peace.

I shared this experience with some of my girlfriends including Jane Wiens, who is wise and very prophetic. She had an interesting take on it:

The basement of a house is the foundation, and this represented a foundation of strength we had built together. The shower and white towel represented purity, holiness, and the innocence of our love for one another. The hug and kiss on his cheek represented covenant and the closeness in our relationship. The smell represented the fragrance of heaven, where he is now.

Bert did not say goodbye – he said he loved me. That meant I would see him again, and it also represented the God's father heart of love for me. The Holy Spirit wanted to show me how much I am loved by God, and He is truly with me every day.

Maybe Bert asked to visit in that dream, to come and encourage me! For a moment, he slipped into my slumber and whispered his heart, like he did in his last days in the hospital.

And it shall come to pass afterward, that I will pour out my Spirit on all flesh; your sons and your daughters shall prophesy, your old men shall dream dreams, and your young men shall see visions. Even on the male and female servants in those days, I will pour out my Spirit.
(Joel 2:28-29)

I Can Feel You

I can feel the distance/deep within the night
I can feel your presence/when I'm walking in the light
I can feel the heavy load when I am far away from you

I can see dark clouds/slowly fade to white
I can feel the loneliness disappearing in the night
When I'm on the narrow road/ I come closer to you.

Chorus: Let the river flow/ Let the strong wind blow
I can feel it/ I can feel you.

I feel the inspiration rise within my soul
Your truth and revelation leading me toward the goal
Have you seen the one I love?
The one I've been searching for.

Chorus: Let the river flow/ Let the strong wind blow
I can feel it/ I can feel you.

Bert Petkau and Chris Janz, *Soldier Boy*, 1998

Hope Nuggets

Hope is the love of friends rooting for your always.

CHAPTER THIRTY

REMEMBERING AND RELEASING

I was meeting my friend Brenda for coffee one day. When we finished, we talked outside for a while, and she said something so moving about Bert.

She had been through a difficult marriage that had ended in divorce, and the scars of that relationship caused her heart to be guarded. She mentioned how Bert always took an interest in people, no matter who they were. With his tender smile and humble presence, he seemingly had all the time in the world for anyone. She said he made her feel comfortable and was always kind and genuinely interested in what she had to say.

It brought tears to my eyes. I thought about many of my female friends who had said the same thing. Bert had a way of making them feel safe. He was charming with a twinkle in his eye, yet not in a way that would ever cross a line. There was a sweet innocence about him that drew you to admire his sincerity.

I thought that was really special, the way he connected with women. He understood them. Perhaps it was because he was raised in a small farming community in Ontario. I remember him telling me that there were more girls his age than boys. He grew up with them, and they were always his friends.

Bert was a man of loyalty in our relationship. Trust and honour were virtues evident in the love we shared with each other. I trusted him completely.

I love that he always took time for people, no matter how busy his schedule was. Bert had a unique way about him, and he was truly one of a kind. You were important; you mattered. People were drawn to him, and he made you feel special.

One night when Bert was hospitalized, he awoke to the sound of sobbing. The patient in the next room had passed away, and his wife and daughter were crying aloud. Bert waited a bit, then rose from his bed and walked feebly to their open door.

The woman was startled to see him and apologized for waking him up. Bert replied that he was more concerned about how they were doing, and he asked if they would feel comfortable coming to his room later so he could pray with them and give them a CD. Perhaps it could ease their sorrow and heartache in some small way.

The mother and daughter stopped by, and Bert did pray for them. Despite the tears, they went away with a small token of comfort. That was my Bert – facing his own painful, dire illness, yet finding the time and compassion to bring comfort to others.

There were hundreds of people praying for Bert all over the world for his body to be healed. Just days before his memorial, there were still people with great faith who came to the funeral home with me to pray for a miracle of healing. I couldn't bring myself to look at him in the casket, so my friend Trish told me how he looked. He looked good. He looked like Bert.

I had such a sense of awe when I entered the room that day. It was a holy moment. Yes, we did have faith and hope, and we did pray together in unity for a miracle. The peace in the room was incredible, and we lingered in it for an hour. As time went on, I eventually felt released to accept the fact that he was gone. I have wondered: When Bert peacefully left this Earth that November afternoon, was it just too good for him to come back?

Bert and I had been living our story, looking forward to many more great years together. I cannot bring him back, and I know he wanted me to move on. We were fortunate to be able to talk about that. During our final days together, we released each other to be free, knowing that one day we will be together again in heaven. It gave me a hope to carry on.

Women of Courage

I think of many women in the Bible, like Esther, Naomi, Ruth, the Samaritan woman at the well, Mary Magdalene and others in those cultures, and of those times, who were not considered to be important.

I love how Jesus spoke to the Samaritan woman, how He revealed himself as the Messiah first to her. He did not reveal himself to the Jewish leaders or the Pharisees. She believed he was the Messiah, and she went on to be probably the first female evangelist.

"Come see a man who told me all that I ever did. Can this be the Christ?" They went out of the town and were coming to him (John 4:29-30 ESV).

Esther found favour in the sight of King Ahasuerus, and was used to save the Jewish people from the deceit of Haman. In the beginning of the story, we are reminded that Esther was an orphan, raised by her uncle, Mordecai. God raised up this ordinary girl to become queen and to save a nation through her humility, patience, and wisdom.

Mary Magdalene, from whom Jesus had cast out seven demons, was present at the crucifixion and prepared his body for burial. She was the first person to whom Jesus appeared on the day of his resurrection. As with Rahab the prostitute, it is interesting how God singled out each of these ordinary women to have a significant place in history, in spite of their difficult beginnings.

We serve a faithful God who turns our sufferings into good (Romans 8:28). And we know that for those who love God; for those who are called according to his purpose, all things work together for good. We must never give in to the struggles we face, no matter how daunting. He is a faithful master who always helps us through. Come with a grateful heart – seeds of discouragement can never take root in a heart that is thankful.

Hope Nuggets

Hope is having the courage to step into the unknown, trusting His arms to catch me.

CHAPTER THIRTY-ONE

DREAMING AGAIN

On our 25th anniversary, Bert and I took that very special trip to Paris that he had promised me so long ago. As we traveled through France and Italy we were in awe of the history and beauty of the land. We dreamed about a return trip to Europe one day.

I recognize that we have been very privileged. Bert's hard work, natural giftedness, willingness to take risks, and the location and era of our working lives have given us opportunities that not everyone has had. We saw our resources as a responsibility from God to be stewarded carefully and to be generous with, but we were very grateful for the chances we've had to enjoy the fruits of our labour as well.

When we traveled, we committed our way to the Lord and were always on the lookout for the ones that God wanted to encourage through us.

Everywhere we went on that trip, we carried a backpack with a bunch of Bert's music CDs. One day when we were having supper in a little restaurant in Monaco, we met a young lady from New York who was on her way to Germany. She was one of 20 young people who had been speaking at a conference on ways her generation could bring unity between German and Jewish youth.

We had a great conversation and admired her courage. Bert pulled out one of his CDs and gave it to her. We felt it was one of those not-by-accident moments, meeting and talking with her.

We took the train back to Nice and the next morning got up early to check out the little town of Eze, famous for French perfumes. As we were wandering through the narrow streets admiring the architecture, we turned a corner and ran into the same young woman we shared supper within Monaco. Of all people! We were all happily surprised.

Things happen for a reason, especially if we ask for our steps to be ordered. Bert and I took the opportunity to encourage this young woman and tell her that she had a strength and a courage within her to bring restoration to a generation looking for hope. That was a special day.

Another time in San Gimignano, we stayed at a farmhouse where we met other travellers and shared life stories around the rustic dinner table. Here, we gave a CD to Erin from Washington, who was an incredible athlete and a world traveler. As we went our separate ways, she and I became Facebook friends.

Out of the blue, almost a year after Bert passed away, I got a message from Erin on my phone with a picture of the *Seven Songs* album. She sent me some kind words and told me how much she loved the CD. She had been going through her own personal struggle, and had come across Bert's music and was playing it. She said the soothing sound of his voice and lyrics were bringing her comfort.

Who would have thought that three years earlier in Italy, giving away a CD would bring solace to someone in need?

Bert and I had begun making plans to see Spain in 2015. He had visited there and other European countries when he was young, and I had a desire to visit Portugal as well. But now, my husband and fellow explorer was gone.

There is a season to mourn the loss of a loved one. It is essential. Still, I knew I could not let a season of mourning become a lifetime thing; I could not let my personal tragedy consume and identify my life.

I could have dwelled in the past. After all, I cherished the life, the love, and the great memories Bert and I shared. Those treasures will always be with me – but not the grief.

There is a time to rise from the ashes and move forward, trusting that God holds a new beginning over the horizon.

I decided that I would stand up to the fear that wanted to keep me paralyzed, helpless, and stuck. I chose to honour the dream Bert and I had, and travel to Spain, without him by my side.

You're My Love Song

You're the voice in the night
You're the whisper in the wind
You're my love song.

You're the light in the dark place
The desire deep within
You're my Love song.

Climb – You're all I want, oh Lord. You're all I need.
There's nothing I want more. You're all I need, Lord.
Chorus – You're my Hope. You're my Rock.
God of my Salvation. You are Life
You are everything.

You're my way. You're my Light
Even in the dark place, you are found
'Cause when love brings heaven down
I can almost hear you. I can hear you.

You're a wonder. You're the warrior
You're the fire that burns within me
You're my love song.

You're the movement. You're the mystery
You're the mercy that I breathe
You're my love song.

Bert Petkau, *Dream*, 2011
https://soundcloud.com/bertpetkau

CHAPTER THIRTY-TWO

AN ADVENTURE IN COURAGE

The first hurdle for me was making all the travel arrangements and itinerary by myself – a new lesson in courage, for sure. I invited Summer to travel with me to Barcelona and then the coast of Portugal for 17 days.

It would be a special trip, continuing on our healing journey and creating cherished memories. I saw the hand of God leading and directing our steps, and I trusted His protection would be over us.

Still, it was the trip that Bert and I had planned but were unable to take together. Summer and I knew that as we looked forward to our flight with both excitement and butterflies in our stomachs.

After a delayed departure and a stopover in Amsterdam, we finally landed in Barcelona, jet-lagged, but well. The next day, we ventured down to our first breakfast of croissants and coffee, and soaked in the sounds of Spanish conversation around us.

As we observed life over the next few days, we noticed how friends greeted each other with a kiss on either cheek. The cultural tradition of honour and respect was obvious. Family was important, and everyone seemed to do things together, young and old – so beautiful.

Down the street from where we were staying was the grand Basílica i Temple Expiatori de la Sagrada Família, the great Roman Catholic Church designed by Gaudí, and a work still in progress today. This was the magnet that had drawn Bert and I so many years ago, and had inspired Bert as a designer and builder.

Summer and I were in awe of its height, and the many cranes working on the outside of this magnificent structure. People lined up for hours to see the inside of the building. That afternoon we got our tickets to go inside and marvel at the colours, lighting, and extraordinary designs within the walls of this masterpiece. I could picture Bert: eyes wide open and impressed by the incredible architectural curves and designs.

Not everything went smoothly on our trip. I was faced with solving travel problems and lugging a heavy suitcase that I would usually have had Bert to help me with. But in spite of these things, Summer and I enjoyed soaking up the atmosphere and the sun in equal measures.

We were hoping for a somewhat cultural experience in the more authentically Spanish places we chose to stay, and somehow managed to communicate through phone translations, sign language, and hand gestures we half understood. So much fun! In the evenings, we walked outside where we saw families eating dinner late at night with small children, even toddlers, playing outside at 10 and 11 p.m. The smiling faces and relaxed atmosphere of family lingered all around.

On one morning, when we were staying in a town on the coast, I got up early for a walk and quiet time, going to the boardwalk along the water. The sun was warm, and the fishermen were throwing out their lines amidst the usual smell of seafood. On my way back, a young woman in her late 20s stopped me and, speaking in perfect English, asked for directions. After four days there, I was familiar with the area and could advise her.

She told me she needed a break from the sun and wanted to see the old city. I told her I was staying there, about a half hour away.

It was easier for her to walk with me than to direct her through the alleys and streets, so we left together.

She was from Austria and studying to be a doctor. As we walked together, she asked me about my holiday, where I was from, and a bit about my life. I told her I was from Canada, that I had children, and why I was in Portugal with my daughter. This led to a conversation about my healing journey and a little about the sudden tragedy of Bert's passing.

She asked me how I was able to cope and said it was courageous for us to be so far from home. She was amazed that I was not angry over Bert's death. Yes, I admitted, I did not understand why he died so young, but my questions would be answered one day. I told her only God gives me peace; He carries me through the difficult days.

We had an amazing conversation, and through it, I was able to share the love, grace, and forgiveness of Jesus Christ. She said she had made a deal with God on this vacation, and wanted to know - was He real? She had such a sweet spirit, and was searching for true meaning in life.

I shared with her how much God loved her. The reason He sent His son into the world was to forgive our sins, and to bring us back into a loving relationship with God the Father.

She took off her sunglasses, and tears were flowing as she looked into my eyes. I said to her, "It was no accident that we met today, and God has a wonderful plan for your life." I also told her she had a gift of compassion, she would become a wonderful doctor, and that this world needed her.

She agreed that we had met for a reason, and God did have a plan for her life. She hugged me, and I felt such a kindred spirit with her even after such a short time together.

It was time to say goodbye. I had to catch a train within the hour. I know in my heart I will see her again one day in eternity. It was a really special moment.

Afterwards, Summer and I prayed for this young woman, and I continued to pray for the land around us as we traveled, asking the Holy Spirit in His way to draw the people to Him. I know "the Word does not return void", and prayer is powerful in travels, even if we don't see the results.

On one of our longer train journeys, Summer and I both had our earbuds in, listening to music and scrolling through photos on our phones, mesmerized as the train made stops along the coastline for passengers to get off and on. Lost in my own little world, I found pictures of Bert that reminded me of the difficult journey we had walked as a family last fall, winter, and spring. I felt a sadness that he was not with me on this trip, and I thought about my healing journey, so far away from home.

I showed Summer some of the pictures, and under our sunglasses, we embraced our heartache as healing tears began to trickle. It was surreal, knowing that even though we were on this magical trip, the pain still lingered. The realities of life still sit at your feet, no matter where you are in the world.

We blotted our tears and tuned in to the beauty before us, gazing out at whitewashed buildings decked with colourful window boxes on wrought iron balconies. A silent moment of grief had touched our hearts, but we turned our thoughts to this beautiful country. I realized, the glitter of the world is so tiny and temporal, while the light of God's presence is brilliant and truly everlasting.

Tears can heal, and it was okay to feel what we had just experienced. I was grateful to be here, and I knew the healing would continue through our adventures in this remarkable land. I knew Jesus was holding our tender hearts close to His, as He continued to minister His love to us.

The trip led me to realize that no matter where we are in life, or in the world, we all need to have hope and purpose. Going overseas did not erase the ache in our hearts, but it did reinforce that we have courage and strength to draw upon each day.

We landed back in Abbotsford to an incredible summer – record-breaking warm days and a season filled with flip-flops, friends, days of walking trails, and lazy evenings at home. It was good to be home sweet home, and in my own bed again.

Hope Nuggets

Hope is the certainty that destiny unfolds treasures every day.

The Petkau girls – Teresa and Summer – on vacation.

CHAPTER THIRTY-THREE

HIKING ON

Summer would often tease her dad and call him "old" (since we had our children in our 30s, that may be considered old for some). She wrote this tribute to her father on his birthday, August 26, 2015, the first birthday after his passing:

Bert Petkau, we hike and we do it in your honour because in your absence we have come to understand why you loved it so much. There's nothing like the feeling you get when you reach the top of a mountain after a gruelling journey. It's worth it. It always will be, and this we have found to be true in life as well. Through the pain, the chaos and the fear, there's always something to look forward to. If only you were here to conquer these mountains with me, Daddy.
Happy 60th Birthday, Old Man! I'll never stop missing you.

I love the fact that many years ago, Bert, Christopher, and Michael, conquered Golden Ears Trail with some friends. It was quite an adventure, and there were even rumours of a black bear along the way.

This hike is a challenging, 12-hour climb. The trail is 24 kilometres top to bottom, and it's a rocky, steep ascent that increases in difficulty. Many hikers camp along the route, taking two days to complete the trek. The park gate closes at night, so there's little time to dally if you attempt it in a day, as my guys did.

I remember Bert and the boys describing the experience as one of the best things they ever did together, and a real accomplishment.

Summer and Sarah climbed many of the mountains and trails in our region after Bert's death. They wanted to honour him, and it also was a way to bring healing to their hearts. They planned to climb Golden Ears on Bert's birthday and were practicing on other trails to prepare for the challenge.

On one of their practice hikes near Vancouver in early May, Sarah twisted her ankle on the way down. Summer was unable to carry her, and Sarah's pain and swelling prompted the girls to stop and rest, hoping someone would come along. Summer told me later that they sat for hours, as few others were on the trail.

I was away at the time, and Summer phoned me later to share their experience. I was praying daily for my family, and she told me how our prayers were answered that day:

A young couple hiking up the mountain finally came by. Of all things, he was a search-and-rescue medic out for leisure with his wife, and they were from Abbotsford, where we lived! They bandaged Sarah's ankle and helped the girls down the mountain – and the four saw no one else during their whole time together.

We counted it to prayer and God's good fathering of Sarah and Summer showing himself faithful when they needed help. Wow – *God is good!* He protects us and answers our prayers.

All of Psalm 91 has been a protective and calming word for me over the years. I meditate on it often and say it out loud. I love how God commissions His angels when we pray; to guard, minister to, and protect us, sometimes even from ourselves. When we call upon Him, He does answer and deliver us from our fears and troubles. When we confidently trust Him to take care of us, He promises to direct the plans and purposes of our lives.

Climbing mountains in our area is adventurous and sometimes difficult, but when we reach the summit, the thrill of getting there and overcoming the physical costs is rewarding. To stand atop a mountain, as I did on Mt. Cheam a few years ago, is a breathtaking moment.

I also conquered Mount Frosty in Manning Park with a friend at another time; a gruelling but lovely 14-kilometre trail. It is gentle at first, but then becomes a 45-degree angle that zigzags with switchbacks partway up. My legs were like rubber the next day, but the experience was well worth it. Sometimes the reward is received on the journey as we realize that we do have an inner strength and courage to do great things in this world.

I think of my friends who are overcoming their battles with cancer now. Brave and courageous women who have drawn from their inner strength and their love of God to help them conquer this disease. It is truly as we embrace the journey of pain that we grow, whatever kind of hurt it is. The pain is temporary, and we don't have to stay there. We can all pass through it.

God will reward us. It is a choice to not settle in the valley, but to climb past it. I am learning in my valleys that there is growth; then mountaintop achievements that become strengthening and memorable milestones in my life.

Daughter Summer celebrates after conquering a Lower Mainland alpine climb.

CHAPTER THIRTY-FOUR

A RIGHT TIME FOR EVERYTHING

The new crispness in the air, rustle of leaves on the ground, and frequent sound of light rain falling confirmed that summer would soon be over. The seasons were changing. There were just a few more chances to mow the lawn and clean up summer debris. My flower baskets of red, yellow and white were losing their colours as autumn found her way into my backyard.

I love my garden, which is lots of work, yet so rewarding. I was a bit afraid of the weed-eater this year, so my nicely lined edges looked a little tattered. Oh well, I got through a beautiful, warm summer mowing and weeding a yard that still managed to look well kept.

I would miss the smell of lavender in my flowerbeds. It brought back memories of the acres of beautiful purple in Provence, that Bert and I had experienced together on our anniversary trip.

I learned that Chris and Sarah would be heading back to the Carolinas before winter and that Summer, a young adult now, would move into her own place with her best friend. This would be her first experience learning to live on her own, paying all her bills, and enjoying independent living.

Where did the time go, when my children were suddenly old enough to leave the comforts of home and venture out on their own?

This was another challenging stretch for me, learning to let my children leave and live their lives. I looked at it as a sign of their healing as they moved forward, creating a future with plans of their own.

Michael lives in the city, and Summer would be nearby, so I was grateful that we would be able to see each other at times. Still, it was not easy, and again I would have to get used to flights, Skype, and messaging. This was all part of His plan. It just came sooner than I expected.

The transition caused me to wonder what was ahead for me. As we get older, it seems right to simplify our lives. Should I sell my house? Should I go somewhere for a fresh start? Should I serve with YWAM in another country, or maybe in Hawaii like my daughter did?

Those thoughts crossed my mind, but I decided not to make any major decisions out of emotion. That's always wise anyway.

I was reminded of something that the late international speaker John Paul Jackson once said, "Peace is the potting soil of revelation." When we are at peace and resting, still and quiet before God, our eyes are opened clearly to know what the Holy Spirit wants us to see, and our ears are fine-tuned to hear what revelation He will give. The spirit of God must be in every choice we make, or it may not be the plan He has for us. There is a right timing when making decisions, and things will fall into place.

This season of suffering was giving me a new understanding of staying close to the Father heart of God and walking in peace. I was learning to understand what it meant to be content, and to trust that God was in control of my life. That made it much easier to rest and let the future unfold for me in due time.

To Wait Upon the Lord

But those who hope in the Lord will renew their strength.
They will soar on wings like eagles; they will run and not grow
weary, they will walk and not be faint.
Isaiah 40:31 (NIV)

This verse speaks of overcoming, courage and strength. How do we obtain the power we need to live day-by-day in this fast-paced life? Hasn't each of us desired to be like the eagle in our battles of life – wishing to mount on wings and soar above our problems, to fly and not grow weary in the mundane routine of life; to walk and not faint when everything around us seems difficult?

Hope Nuggets

Hope is the strength of an eagle rising above the storms.

CHAPTER THIRTY-FIVE

PURPOSE

My mom is 93 years old. She is a true overcomer, a faithful woman of prayer, and she still drives in the daytime, goes to the gym, and also loves her garden. She loves to pray for people too and has been an incredible blessing to many. It's hard to believe she outlived Bert.

I was having a visit with my mom and we were talking about purpose – that if people don't have purpose, something dies inside of them.

I thought about that for a minute and realized how true that is. We all need a purpose. God created each one of us with gifts and his plan for us is to know what our gifts are and to use those gifts here on Earth for the benefit of others. It starts with understanding that God has designed us uniquely.

When I was in my twenties, I worked for a really good company. I made good money, travelled, and bought a great sports car – which eventually turned into the down payment on our first home. But not long after I married Bert, I decided to stop working, and people thought I was crazy to give up good benefits and seniority.

I did have a purpose in that season of my life: I felt it was time to be a mom. I wanted to stay home and raise my children, to be there for them during each stage of their young lives.

This was now my new purpose – to be a wife and mother.

My husband was a gifted man. He invented many different construction products for high rises and commercial buildings. God gave Bert the ideas and intuition to devise his inventions and a purpose for each of them. Bert invested his time, energy and dedication into using these gifts as God led him.

Successes in life do not happen overnight. I remember when Bert and I lived in a small apartment with our two little boys, and he would come home from work with cement in his hair and his clothes – almost impossible to launder out. In those early days, through rain and mud, character was developing in our hearts. Over time, through perseverance, our company grew one small step at a time. It took prayer, patience and wisdom for Bert's gifts to develop and for our company to become successful after many years. Bert was fulfilling his purpose in business and in his spiritual life through his faithfulness.

Recently, on Father's Day, my kids and I were walking along a street in Vancouver and we passed a new structure about eight stories high. My son Chris noticed the blue liner cones his dad had invented in the forms on that job, and we looked at each other and smiled.

My daughter-in-law Sarah is a really gifted makeup artist. Last summer at a family get-together, she did my makeup. It was fun getting pampered, and she made me look great with her contouring skills. The sweet thing was, while she was doing this, she had a huge smile on her face! She was passionate about what she was doing.

Some people are gifted musicians, artists, teachers, investors, builders, athletes, scientists or ministers – the list goes on. God has created each one of us so uniquely. If we enjoy what we do, it's fulfilling and brings meaning to life.

In the post-Bert season of my life, I am no longer defined

by my roles of wife and mother. Although I still want to provide a place for my kids to gather and reconnect, I have needed to understand what my focus is to be now. What is my purpose?

Sometimes it's useful to have other people help you to see yourself more clearly. My friend Lisa describes me as an encourager and a life coach. Each day I look forward to having conversations about life with the people I encounter, and encouraging them to discover who God has created them to be. I can also see that the blessing on my mom's life to pray, has been passed down to me and I believe will also be passed to my children one day. I want to see that blessing grow in me.

Neither of these gifts is concrete, or measurable, or even visible to the outside world. But inside my heart, I have the joy of knowing my purpose.

The Lord will fulfill his purpose for me: your steadfast love, O Lord, endures forever. Do not forsake the work of your hands. (Psalm 138:8)

All things work together for good for those that are called according to His purpose. (Romans 8:28)

Hope Nuggets

Hope lifts our eyes heavenward to embrace God's tender glance.

CHAPTER THIRTY-SIX

CHALLENGED

I met my friend Lee Anne Hanson back at Bert's CD release party. I happened to sit next to her as the band was practicing for the event, and it was our first encounter.

I soon learned that Bert and Lee were like kindred spirits – a brother and sister in the Lord. She later told me stories about Bert sharing with her his many ideas, his love for God, and his heart for unity.

Lee spent many days in our home and the hospital crying out for God to bring healing to Bert. She would send me hopeful emails, and she became a constant in my life in those difficult days.

After Bert passed away, we got together regularly to share our hearts and begin to pray together for our city. She would say to me in her beautiful South African accent: "I can't believe Bert's gone. I sure miss our talks." I could picture him with a twinkle in his eye, sharing his ideas, and how excited he would be about each of them!

One time after visiting and praying with Lee, I was driving home, and happened to be following a black Tundra truck. As I went up the hill to pass it, I instinctively looked in at the driver – only to realize, it was not Bert. Lee said that she, too, would see a black Tundra and impulsively glance to see if it was him.

We sure missed Bert. But, as the months passed by, the grief lessened, and we were gradually able to look to heaven in peace and ask, "Bert, why did you have to leave us now?"

That September, Lee and I went to Vancouver to hear a speaker from the International House of Prayer (IHOP) in Kansas City. Getting a house of prayer and worship in Abbotsford was something that had been on many of our hearts. (We hope one day this will become a reality.)

The room was filled with people of Chinese descent who have a heart for Vancouver and surrounding areas. They knew how to worship, and they knew how to pray. Lee introduced me to one of them, her sweet friend Joy, a lady probably in her mid-60s. She radiated the love of Jesus, and when she took my hand in hers, I felt such warmth and kindness.

Joy used to travel with a man named "Watchman Nee." He wrote books that I read in the early 1980s, and they really impacted my life. Some of them were The Spiritual Man; Sit, Walk, Stand; and The Normal Christian Life.

Watchman was a man who was sold out for the sake of the gospel. He lived a life dedicated to ministering in China beginning in the 1920s. He was persecuted for sharing his beliefs during the Communist takeover, and he died in prison in 1972.

God used him mightily in his lifetime. Joy, the little lady beside me that night, not only travelled with Watchman and his ministry, but also was a powerful intercessor herself.

After the message had been shared, I watched as she knelt with a box of Kleenex, gently crying for the mercy of God for the people of Vancouver.

I was in awe. Being with such seasoned people who were sold out for Jesus truly ministered to me. To be in God's presence and with His children who have lived lives of true abandonment for His sake was humbling. I was challenged in my understanding of the power and the promise of prayer and felt a new strength and courage rise up in me.

My friend James Schafer once said: "A thousand trickling hearts, and you have a gently flowing stream. Ten gently flowing streams, and you have a large filling pool. Three large filling pools and our valley can be flooded with the presence of God's love."

Just like that picture of the hearts flowing together, Bert's dream was to see believers in our area united so they could fulfill the plans of God in their own lives and in the nations. I still carry that dream in my heart and want to stand strong and agree with God in prayer for this to happen.

Hope Nuggets

The three remain: Faith Hope and Love.

CHAPTER THIRTY-SEVEN

A YEAR GONE BY

My year of firsts – facing each memory and the painful anniversaries around my life with Bert – came to completion. I went away for five days to embrace the month of November and contemplate the dates that were especially significant in this difficult time of my life: November 7 - our last anniversary together; 17 - Bert's last day on earth; and 27 - when our friends and family gathered to say goodbye.

Warm sun and the company of a special girlfriend helped me process and accept each of these days. When I returned home, I sensed that a deep sadness had tangibly lifted off me. It really felt like a large measure of grief had been purged through my journey. My heart no longer ached.

I was grateful for release from the sharp pain and for the knowledge that someday there would be no more tears.

The number seven represents completion – God rested on the seventh day of his creating. It felt like the beautiful passage of 27 years with my special man had been completed. He had received his miracle of healing in a different way than we had been hoping for, but was now pain-free and enjoying life in eternity.

I had noticed a "sign" twice in a number of days that summer when I sat outside on my balcony looking at the magnificence of God's creation. Stunning Mount Baker looked back at me in its snowcapped majesty.

It was in this setting that I saw several eagles soar past, one-by-one, and circle upward high above. I counted them as they glided by and was amazed to see seven of those glorious birds together. The timing of their presence was significant: God was showing me that he had me in mind in this healing season of my life – and was completing his good work in me.

An eagle can detect a storm when it is approaching, long before it arrives. It will fly to a high spot and wait for winds to lift it safely above the tempest. I am learning like the eagle that there is a way to rise above the storms – into God's presence, into his peace, and into a new hope for the future.

Bert – the dreamer, full of ideas – is with the cloud of witnesses cheering me on. As my daughter said: "Mom, Dad would be so proud of you, and the good decisions you've made without him by your side."

The very first item Bert put into our new home in March 2014 was a plaque that said, "As For Me And My House We Will Serve the Lord." *(Joshua 24:15)* Our promise to serve the God of Abraham, Isaac, and Jacob – no matter what happens – has been a privilege, and still stands. And His promise to be with us always has been proven over and over. He is my life, He is my source, and He is my Hope.

Live Like That

Sometimes I think
What will people say of me
When I'm only just a memory
When I'm home where my soul belongs

Was I love
When no one else would show up
Was I Jesus to the least of those
Was my worship more than just a song

I want to live like that
And give it all I have
So that everything I say and do
Points to You

If love is who I am
Then this is where I'll stand
Recklessly abandoned
Never holding back

I want to live like that
I want to live like that
I am I am proof
That You are who you say You are
That grace can really change a heart
Do I live like Your love is true

People pass
And even if they don't know my name
Is there evidence that I've been changed
When they see me, do they see You
I want to live like that
And give it all I have
So that everything I say and do
Points to You

If love is who I am
Then this is where I'll stand
Recklessly abandoned
Never holding back

I want to live like that
I want to live like that

I want to show the world the love You gave for me
I'm longing for the world to know the glory of the King

I want to live like that
And give it all I have
So that everything I say and do
Points to You

If love is who I am
Then this is where I'll stand
Recklessly abandoned
Never holding back

I want to live like that
I want to live like that,
I want to live like that

Sidewalk Prophets:
David Douglas Frey, Ben McDonald and Ben Glover
Used with permission

> Fear not, for I am with you;
> be not dismayed, for I am your God;
> I will strengthen you, I will help you,
> I will uphold you with my righteous right hand.
> For I, the Lord your God, hold your right hand;
> it is I who say to you, "Fear not,
> I am the one who helps you."
> (Isaiah 41:10, 13)

CHAPTER THIRTY-EIGHT

POSTSCRIPT

A lot has happened in the two years since I commemorated the end of my first year alone. I have continued to heal, grow, take risks, and be stretched. I have also been finding joy in the journey and seeing God's faithfulness every step of the way.

I saw it when I began thinking about getting a job. I hadn't officially been in the workforce for over 30 years except to help Bert with our business. I don't have a diploma. I do have an unfinished bachelor's degree with lots of liberal arts courses, which may not amount to much these days.

I was not sure what I was qualified for, but I was talking to a friend one day and she casually mentioned she was looking for a part-time receptionist at the engineering firm that she and her husband owned. A few weeks later, I drove out for the interview with no idea what to expect – and I was hired!

Yay! I love my job and the people I work with. It's incredible what I have learned and how rewarding it is – and the strength it has brought to my self-esteem.

Then, near the end of 2016, I saw God's faithfulness in the way he led me to sell my home and move into a "me-sized" townhouse. God was so good to direct me to the right place in a really tight market and show me the optimal time to sell the home that Bert and I had built together. God really is "a father to the fatherless, and defender of widows." (Psalm 65:5)

I also saw God's faithfulness recently on a beautiful sunny September afternoon when Summer and the special young man that she had met in Kona got married. (Another American stole another one of my kids! It's okay, I love the USA.)

I recalled my thoughts around the time of Bert's illness when I realized that he wouldn't be around to walk his daughter down the aisle. We decided that Chris and Michael would take Bert's place and that the three of us together would give her away. What bittersweet emotions! My boys sat on either side of me during the vows, and it was as if the Father himself comforted me when Chris put his arm around me for the rest of the service. I felt such peace and could fully enter in.

To experience watching two young people truly in love, and the power of God's love upon this special union was magical.

My Purpose Grows

God's faithfulness has also been evident as he has given me several opportunities to follow my heart's desire to engage with prayer communities.

One of these opportunities was a road trip with good friends to visit Bethel Church in Redding, California. The Bethel atmosphere was alive with people who have learned to honour one another and treat each other with respect. Those who attend Bethel make a huge difference in their community. They clean up streets, minister to the poor and broken, and have been recognized by the city for changing the atmosphere and culture of the area.

One reason I wanted to go to Bethel was to visit the healing rooms and allow the Holy Spirit to minister to my heart. I sat in a large auditorium waiting for my turn. Despite the activity, I was with awesome stillness. When my number was called, and I went to the next room where smiling faces greeted me and healers gently put their hands upon my back to minister the love of our heavenly Father.

The next day we attended a Sunday service. Just before the band was to start, my friend Lee recognized the worship leader, Jeremy Riddle, a well-known young man in his early 30s. Lee went to the stage to speak with him, and within seconds he came over to where we were seated. Jeremy, Joyce, Lee and I held hands as he prayed a blessing over the vision Bert and I had: "Dream City."

Jeremy's songs were marvellous, stunningly sung from a heart of true passion for the Lord Jesus Christ. The words and lyrics touched the heartstrings of the soul. We each came away with a renewal – some physical and emotional healing – that carried us back home to B.C. like a gentle, refreshing wind.

The Call

A few months later, I had the privilege of attending Lou Engle's "The Call", which marked 110 years since a famous outpouring of the Holy Spirit came upon people praying in the Azusa section of Los Angeles.

The Azusa Street Revival was led by African-American preacher William J. Seymour and gave birth to the Pentecostal movement. The revival began on April 9, 1906, and continued for almost a decade. There were signs, wonders and healings, and a generation of people supernaturally changed by the presence of God.

Engle is an American Christian leader who envisioned another move of God on the anniversary of the Azusa phenomenon. He imagined a similar outpouring of the Holy Spirit upon the hearts and minds of people not only in North America but also around the world.

I booked my flight with my friends Judy and Joyce who shared the same desire to be a part of a worldwide movement of prayer. We headed to Los Angeles where up to 100,000 others were expected to attend the event at Memorial Coliseum.

We arrived to discover we were booked in a house across the street because all rooms in the estate were full. Our host led us to a small room with two bunk beds. When we saw a suitcase and groceries under one of the beds, we wondered who our mystery guest was. Later that evening we found out that she was a young woman from Frankfurt, Germany.

Karine worked in television there and was on holiday for a few weeks, exploring museums, beaches, and Hollywood. We shared our Azusa experiences with her each day, and soon the three of us built a lovely friendship with her – God's plan at work.

A couple of days later, Karine was leaving to another part of L.A., and we three had a wonderful, moving opportunity to pray with her and bless her. With tears in her eyes, she embraced Jesus Christ as her Saviour!

The Call became a history-making event with tens of thousands of believers gathering in accord, despite rain showers throughout the day. Repentance, forgiveness, worship and prayer rang out as the throng called to God for an outpouring of mercy and grace. Such a significant time for me!

As this manuscript is in its final stage of proofreading, I am celebrating what would have been Bert's and my 30th wedding anniversary. Today I am missing Bert, experiencing grief, and thinking about 'what could have been'. These feelings aren't as devastating as they used to be, and they don't dominate my existence, but I know they will continue to come from time to time. When they do, I will continue to give them to the Lord and receive His comfort.

In the midst of this reality, I look forward to the future with joy, as I follow the One who cares for me. God truly has a destiny for each one of us. As I continue to stay close to Him, He is orchestrating a plan better than anything I could have dreamed would come from my heartache, just a few short years ago. Like the lyrics in Bert's song "So Loved": Turn your hearts to heaven, for you are so loved. Yes, know you are loved. **Know that God Can take ashes and turn them into a beautiful story of hope.**

To contact me to share my story of hope.
contact: **teresapetkau@gmail.com**

So Loved

You can hide away but when you turn your eyes
Let your heart be stirred to heaven
You can feel strong when you feel love burn within
Let your heart be stirred to heaven

Let your heart be stirred (cause you are so loved)
Let your heart be stirred
Let your heart be stirred forever and always

Can you see, can you feel it. Here it comes again
Let your heart be stirred to heaven
Can you see can you feel his love reaching out
Let your heart be stirred to heaven
Let your heart be stirred cause you are so loved
Let your heart be stirred forever and always

Hey,hey, hey, Ohh ohh,ohh
Heaven waits for you
Heaven waits for you
Hey,hey, hey, Ohh,ohh,ohh

This I know is true
Heaven waits for you
Hey,hey,hey, Ohh,ohh,ohh
No matter what you're going through
Can you feel His love for you

**Bert Petkau, sung by Stephanie Antonio, *Lights &
Oceans,* 2014**
http://www.soundcloud.com/bertpetkau

ACKNOWLEDGEMENTS

There were are so many people who walked through this journey with my family and me in the fall and winter months of 2014. Also, as the dust began to settle in 2015, many of you continued to be there for us on the road to healing. THANK YOU!

To my children – Christopher, Michael, and Summer – you are strong and courageous, and I pray for you always. God promised me He would look after the fatherless, and I know he will.

To my daughter-in-law Sarah Petkau, for being a good friend to me.

To my Mom, who is 94 and has faithfully prayed for my family for many years.

To my siblings, who reached out in love during the hard days at the hospital and afterward.

To Jay Nivers and Misty Bedwell, who helped me organize my ideas for this book and helped me start putting it all together.

To April Bartsch, my editor, and good friend, for the many days and hours of editing. Her gift of bringing my story to life is evident in the excellent way she fine-tuned the details of this journal. Love you girl.

Win and Carrie Wachsmann When it was time to find a publisher our paths crossed and it was perfect timing, thank you.

Dan and Sandy Thiessen As the years went by you counselled me with wisdom,kindness and love. thank you

To Lorraine Dunne, Bert's sister, who is my sister and friend.

To Bruce and Trish Warren, who prayed for a healing miracle for Bert to the very end.

To Dean Maerz, who became a brother and close friend throughout the year 2015.

To Leeanne Hanson-Nivers, who (with Dean) was a pillar of wisdom and strength for me throughout 2015.

Thank you to David and Lisa Lowndes, who walked faithfully with me and let me hang out with them on many, many weekends. Love you guys.

To Doug and Suzie Watts, Judy and Phil Bowler, and Kenny Rahn, who prayed for Bert at home and in the hospital. Kenny, thank you for your worship times with Bert.

To Andre and Steph Antonio and Steph's brother-in-law, Dave, for your times of worship and prayers, constantly ministering to us in the hospital. Andre and Steph, my prayer is that you will continue to bless many with the gift of music God has placed within you both, and that lives will be changed through you.

To Ruben Friesen and Joan Klassen, thank you for taking the helm for BCC.

To Steve and Marion Bradner, who faithfully prayed for me and sent encouraging texts. I feel your prayers covering my home and my family.

To Gord Unger and Scott Webster, my accountants, and Brad Willems at Assante Investments, for assisting me with all the ongoing business concerns.

To April Klassen, who reached out to me at the beginning of this journey.

To David Kim, for traveling from South Korea to minister to us as a family.

To Ron Peters, thank you for capturing such special memories for us as a family.

To John and Diane Van Vloten, for standing with me when I could barely stand myself.

To Leah Holmes, Dan Madden, Marvin Bargen, Albert Janzen, Andrew DeKezel and others who have repaired things in my home.

To Vi Wiens, Angie Janzen, Joyce Grubb, and Judy MacDonald, my partners in crime in a very good way, on our ministry nights.

To the Wednesday night prayer group who stand with me in prayer for the vision God gave to Bert and me for Dream City.

Thank you to all who took the time to come visit Bert and I in our home, or visited in the hospital, and stood steadfast with us in prayer all over the world. Thank you for the faithful prayers of our friends serving in various Youth With a Mission centres around the world.

Thank you to my neighbours, family, and friends who made meals for us when we could hardly function. And THANK YOU for having me over for dinner on those difficult nights!

Thank you to all of you who helped with or came to Bert's celebration of life, and for all the beautiful flowers, notes and cards now safely tucked away.

Thank you to all of my Facebook friends near and far – who sent encouraging words in that year of firsts and continued to do so in the days that followed – for all your prayers of love, comfort, and kindness.

Today I honour Bert and my good friend whom I mention in my story Leeanne Hanson-Nivers. She passed away two days after what would have been my 30th wedding anniversary on November 09, 2017. She fought a courageous three year battle with a restrictive lung disease. I miss you my sister and sweet friend. I'm glad you are rejoicing in heaven with Bert and the others we love.

Thank you to all of you whose paths have crossed with mine in this journey. Your prayers and words of encouragement, loving us and standing with us through this difficult journey will never be forgotten.

ABOUT THE AUTHOR

When life throws those unexpectant curveballs your way, ones you never thought would turn your life upside down and change a destiny that would end up becoming an adventure of a life time. Hope is the anchor that turned my tragedy from despair into a courage I never new was deep within my soul. We all experience loss of some kind and it is how we get through the loss that counts. In a world of hopelessness, people are longing for hope. My testimony of faith will light up your heart to embrace the journey each one of us walks every day. I found a peace and strength like no other that has carried me to a new place offering hope to those who cross my path every day. I want to awaken the heart to a deeper, joyous grace through a love that has captured my heart and I am excited to share with you.

Teresa Petkau is an inspiring woman of prayer and through her journey longs to see people set free from hopelessness. She is carrying on a legacy her and her late husband desired to see unity within the church body and people fulfilling their own unique destinies. She shares a story of comfort and encouragement that through the most difficult storms of life like an eagle one can soar above the chaos and in the eye of the storm find peace. This testimony is a love story as well as a promise that the successes in life come through courage, never giving up and trusting God through his grace He will come through every time. Teresa has three children and lives in Abbotsford B.C.

You may contact Teresa at:
teresapetkau@gmail.com

Made in the USA
San Bernardino, CA
18 February 2018